Keeping Religious Institutions Secure

Keeping Religious Institutions Secure

Jennie-Leigh McLamb
Independent Security Consultant
Richmond/Fredericksburg
Virginia, USA

Amsterdam • Boston • Heidelberg • London • New York • Oxford
Paris • San Diego • San Francisco • Singapore • Sydney • Tokyo
Butterworth-Heinemann is an imprint of Elsevier

Butterworth-Heinemann is an imprint of Elsevier
The Boulevard, Langford Lane, Kidlington, Oxford OX5 1GB, UK
225 Wyman Street, Waltham, MA 02451, USA

Notices
Knowledge and best practice in this field are constantly changing. As new research and
experience broaden our understanding, changes in research methods, professional practices, or
medical treatment may become necessary.

Practitioners and researchers must always rely on their own experience and knowledge in
evaluating and using any information, methods, compounds, or experiments described herein.
In using such information or methods they should be mindful of their own safety and the
safety of others, including parties for whom they have a professional responsibility.

To the fullest extent of the law, neither the Publisher nor the authors, contributors, or editors,
assume any injury and/or damage to persons or property as a matter of products liability,
negligence or otherwise, or from any use or operation of any methods, products, instructions,
or ideas contained in the material herein.

ISBN: 978-0-12-801346-5

British Library Cataloguing in Publication Data
A catalogue record for this book is available from the British Library

Library of Congress Cataloging-in-Publication Data
A catalog record for this book is available from the Library of Congress

For Information on all Butterworth-Heinemann publications
visit our website at http://store.elsevier.com/

Printed and bound in the USA

Working together
to grow libraries in
developing countries

www.elsevier.com • www.bookaid.org

Contents

About the Authors

Jennie-Leigh McLamb, CPP, PSP, PCI, has over 12 years of experience in private security. She worked in the Private Security Services Section of Virginia's Department of Criminal Justice Services (DCJS) where she performed a variety of functions including evaluating sources for alternative training credit, conducting compliance agent training, and helping develop new regulations as well as internal policies and procedures for regulating private security personnel. As Compliance and Training Administrator for nine years at a private security firm, she managed training and licensing of over 1500 individuals across multiple jurisdictions and contract requirements, designed and updated curriculum and tests, and developed training plans in support of business proposals. She was an instructor and curriculum developer for both online and onsite courses in various security topics including access control, patrol, confrontation management, and others.

She has an MS in Security Management and is finishing an MBA with concentrations in Cybersecurity and Information Security Management. She also has an MA in Anthropology. She earned all three ASIS International security certifications in 2012: Certified Protection Professional (CPP), Physical Security Professional (PSP), and Professional Certified Investigator (PCI).

Since January 2014, she has worked as an Independent Security Consultant who provides expertise in the following areas: curriculum development, physical security surveys, risk assessments, developing policies and procedures, training assessments, and other security topics.

David Binkley, PSP, has over 10 years of experience in physical security, firearms handling and training, and use of less-lethal weapons. A former Marine, he was a Marine Corps Martial Arts Instructor and a member of the Silent Drill Team. In 2011, he earned the ASIS International Physical Security Professional (PSP) certification.

Since 2005, he has performed as a cleared armed access control officer for a high-level government agency to include but not limited to the following: property access control, building protection, traffic control, inspect vehicles, assist visitors, perform roving patrol, enforce regulation, report breaches of security, ability to respond to emergency situations including pursuit, apprehension and detention of individuals, monitoring of alarm and CCTV.

An instructor since 2006, he has trained military, police, government, and contract security officers in close quarter combat, special weapons and tactics, defensive tactics, low-light shooting, ballistic shield training, pistol qualification, shotgun qualifications, and long-range rifle qualifications. He is a certified instructor of security officers in basic, advanced handgun, shotgun, and precision rifle

techniques. He possesses instructor certifications from the National Rifle Association (NRA), Virginia's Department of Criminal Justice Services (DCJS), Sig Arms,
and the Ohio Peace Officers Training Academy (OPOTA).

He also earned armorer certificates in the following weapon systems: Glock,
Remington 870, Beretta, Smith & Wesson M&P, Sig Arms, Springfield Armory, and
Colt.

Preface

Religious violence has been on the rise around the world. Groups like ISIS and Boko Haram have perpetrated terrorist acts against members of other religious traditions. This includes destruction of religious iconography, damage to property and buildings, and killing those who refuse to convert. Sectarian violence—violence between sects of the same major tradition—has also been on the rise.

The increased visibility of religious terrorists, as well as active shooters at the workplace or school, may encourage copycat crimes. It is imperative for religious institutions to prepare for the potential of violent acts.

Unfortunately, faith is not enough to protect followers of religious traditions from the possibility of violent acts perpetrated against them. Religious institutions need to change their way of thinking.

The idea for this book was generated by news reports of violence at religious institutions. As I considered these events, I discovered that there were few resources dedicated to the unique needs of religious institutions and designed for the specific audience of non-security personnel. My hope is that religious institutions will use the information in this book to protect their attendees, employees, and facility.

Acknowledgments

I would like to thank David Binkley for writing the following chapters: Chapter 16 Keeping the Principal Safe and Chapter 17 Assessing the Need for Less Lethal Tools and Firearms. His expertise was invaluable in writing these chapters.

I would also like to thank my husband and my parents for their support, encouragement, and patience. Without them, this book would not have been possible.

Finally, I would also like to thank a few more individuals who have contributed to my knowledge and understanding of security principles: Lynn H. Herring, David A. Long, Sr., Burton Walker, and Robbie Robertson. Their mentorship, expertise, and support have been instrumental in my development as a security professional.

Introduction

1

Religious institutions—whether they are a temple, mosque, synagogue, church, or other structure—are considered by their attendees to be a sanctuary that provides a safe refuge from the troubles of the outside world. They are a place to worship, sing, praise, contemplate, and enjoy fellowship with other believers. They are welcoming places that provide guidance, healing, support, and comfort in times of need. As a result, most attendees see them as sacred places. Unfortunately, criminals see them as an easy, target-rich environment.

The FBI's Uniform Crime Report http://www.fbi.gov/about-us/cjis/ucr does not separate religious institutions from other businesses, making precise numbers difficult to ascertain.[1] However, it is known that religious institutions are often victimized more than once and usually within a short period of time.[2] In one instance, a church had their sound equipment stolen. A few weeks after replacing the equipment, the place was hit again, and the new sound equipment was stolen.[3]

Incidents in the United States

A brief listing of crimes in religious institutions shows the scope of the problem.

- March 2005: A gunman killed eight people including himself at a church meeting—of which he was a member—in a Sheraton Hotel in Milwaukee, Wisconsin.[4]
- August 2012: A gunman killed six people and wounded four at a Sikh temple in Oak Creek, Wisconsin.[5]
- July 2008: A 58-year-old man entered a Unitarian Universalist Church and opened fire. Nine people were shot, and two were killed. Police arrived within 3 min, but three members had already subdued the shooter.[6]
- February 2010: Three gunmen opened fire during a service at New Gethsemane Church of God in Christ in California, wounding two people.[7]
- A nun was strangled in a church garden.[8]
- A pastor was shot in his front yard for counseling the abused wife of a violent husband.[9]
- An emotionally disturbed man took a congregation hostage and held them in a confrontation with police.[10]
- A deranged man drove his truck through the church doors during services.[11]
- A woman, who was praying, was assaulted, robbed, and raped in the sanctuary.[12]

There are several sources of information on religious violence that can be found on the internet. Carl Chinn also tracks deadly force incidents in religious institutions on his Website www.carlchinn.com. Another Website with information on events from history to the present is maintained by Ontario Consultants on Religious Tolerance. It can be found at http://www.religioustolerance.org/intol_news.htm. The Center for the Study of Religious

Violence has a Website with blog at http://religiousviolence.wordpress.com/, which contains articles and links relating to incidents of religious violence around the globe.

As these incidents show, no religious tradition or denomination is immune to violence. Facilities in every state, whether the city is large or small, are vulnerable. These are just a few of the reported incidents. It is estimated that most incidents go unreported.

Incidents Outside the United States

Religious institutions outside the United States have experienced dramatic events as well. Many countries are known for incidents of religious violence, particularly clashes between different religions, as well as clashes between different denominations of the same religion. The U.S. State Department issues an International Religious Freedom Report that describes the status of religious freedom in each foreign country, government policies violating religious belief and practices of groups, religious denominations, and individuals, and US policies to promote religious freedom around the world. The 2012 report can be accessed at http://www.state.gov/j/drl/rls/irf/religiousfreedom/index.htm.

According to a Pew Center Report, religious hostilities around the world reached a six-year high in 2012.[13] The level of harassment or intimidation of particular religious groups also experienced an increase in 2012. Harassers were governments—national, provincial, or local—as well as individuals and groups. Christians were harassed in 110 countries and Muslims in 109.[14] In addition, 2012 also saw an increase in the share of countries where violence or the threat of violence was used to compel adherence to religious norms.[15] The full study can be viewed at http://www.pewforum.org/2014/01/14/religious-hostilities-reach-six-year-high/.

- December 2012: At least 12 were killed in attacks on two Nigerian churches.[16]
- August 2013: The Greek Catholic Mar Elias Church and the Sunni Muslim Grand Mosque in Qusayr, Syria, were both almost totally destroyed as government and rebel forces battled for control. Though some icons have been recovered, they suffered grievous damage, with burns and tears running through the gilded works of art.[17]
- October 2013: Forty Coptic Christian Churches were attacked in Egypt.[18]
- June 2014: Hard-line Buddhists hurled gasoline bombs and looted homes and businesses on a Sunday in several towns in southwestern Sri Lanka. The attacks were led by a mob from Bodu Bala Sena (Buddhist Power Force), which rails against the country's Muslim minority.[19]

Terminology

To avoid confusion, the following terms will be used throughout this book. I've attempted to keep them as religion-neutral as possible so as to apply to a broad spectrum of religious traditions and organizational structures.

- **Facility** refers to the physical building and grounds, whether it is a temple, mosque, synagogue, church, parochial school, or other religious building.
- **Organization** refers to the group as a whole, including facility, the staff, and members.

—Cont'd

- **Principal** refers to the head person at the facility. This person has the final say on all decisions made for the facility and its attendees, although he/she may listen to a council or group of advisors.
- **Leaders** refer to formal or informal religious specialists such as clerics, pastors, priests, monks, rabbis, imams, ministers, and preachers who are typically ordained or otherwise designated as religious authorities by a certifying body, the audience, or the principal.
- **Advisors** are those **leaders** who have positions of authority within the religious tradition and who advise the principal. Advisors may include deacons, elders, bishops, and monks.
- **Audience**, used interchangeably with **attendees**, refers to the people who adhere to a particular religious tradition and attend a specific facility in order to worship.
- **Administrators** are those people such as office managers, secretaries, or assistants who work for the **principal** and other **leaders** in secular positions. They are also called **staff** or **employees**.
- **Volunteers** are those who work in various capacities as needed but do not receive monetary compensation for their work.
- **Adversary** is anyone who poses a threat to the organization, facility, or its people regardless of motive, action, or method. This term is used interchangeably with **perpetrator**.

Safety versus Security

Often used interchangeably, the terms "safety" and "security" actually have different meanings in the context of this book. Safety refers to the absence of danger, whereas security refers to the ability to manage or mitigate danger.[20]

Typically, safety refers to the operations of systems in abnormal environments—such as flood, fire, earthquake, electrical faults, or accidents. Security refers to those systems that are used to prevent or detect an attack by a malevolent human adversary.[21]

Purpose and Scope of this Book

This book is not an attempt to question anyone's faith, but it is intended to provide additional tools that can be utilized so attendees are free to worship as they choose without fear of crime or violence. This book is designed to provide religious intuitions with a basic understanding of risk, methods of protection, and other considerations they need to take into account in order to keep their facility, property, and users secure. Whenever possible, it is important to consult and/or hire professionals who can provide the proper information on systems for lighting, access control, and intrusion detection.

Organization of this Book

This book is organized as a logical progression from basic security principles to planning to respond to an incident to recovering from one. It also takes into account special issues such as handling at-risk individuals, considerations for children and youth, and lesser known but potentially devastating effects such as loss of reputation and liability issues.

Considerations

In order to keep your facility, staff, and attendees secure, there are several things to keep in mind. First, you must recognize that crime can and does happen in religious institutions and that they are a target-rich environment. It is important to remember that "people are more at risk when they feel they are safest."[22] This is because they let their guard down and may not pay attention to signs of trouble.

Security starts months before you even realize an incident may occur. As with an emergency or crisis, preparedness and planning are essential to a successful resolution of the incident. There is no single answer to the problem of violence in religious institutions. A complex and multifaceted issue, it requires extensive training, thorough planning, and consistency in implementation. A variety of strategies must be used that take into account the unique needs of the particular institution(s) with which you are concerned. Administrators, staff, and attendees need to work together to ensure a safe and secure environment. You cannot do it all, and you cannot do it alone.

Police are reactive; you need to be proactive and prepare for a potential event. Security does not have to be armed guards and metal detectors. There are many things you can do to create a safe and secure environment without contributing to an atmosphere of fear. There is a natural conflict between convenience and security. However, a balance must be maintained between the institution's mission and security measures.

"Security and safety are issues that, if not implemented properly, can create disunity and division because they alter the way your congregation does business. However, crime prevention strategies can be implemented smoothly and professionally, with little impact on the congregation. Many of our recommendations can occur with little change and without disrupting your regular method of worship."[23]

Despite the challenge of recognizing potential threats, there are ways to prevent, mitigate, and respond to them. There is no surefire way to guarantee a peaceful resolution, but we can provide you with tools to contribute to the successful handling of violent or criminal acts or events at your facility.

End Notes

1. Quarles C. L. and Ratliff P. L., *Crime Prevention for Houses of Worship* (Alexandria: American Society for Industrial Security, 2001).
2. Ibid.
3. Ibid.

4. Sinai J., *Active Shooter: A Handbook on Prevention* (Alexandria: ASIS International, 2013).
5. Ibid.
6. Blair J. P. et al., *Active Shooter Events and Response* (Boca Raton: CRC Press, 2013).
7. Burk T., Weiss J. and Davis M., "Church Protectors," *The Journal of Counterterrorism and Homeland Security International* 20, no. 2 (2014): 36–39.
8. See note 1 above, p. 4.
9. Ibid.
10. Ibid.
11. Ibid.
12. Ibid.
13. http://www.pewforum.org/2014/01/14/religious-hostilities-reach-six-year-high/.
14. Ibid.
15. Ibid.
16. See note 7 above.
17. http://www.huffingtonpost.com/2013/08/06/syria-conflict-destroys-mosques-churches_n_3709262.html.
18. See note 7 above.
19. See note 17 above.
20. See note 7 above.
21. Garcia M. L., *The Design and Evaluation of Physical Protection Systems*, Second Edition (Massachusetts: Butterworth-Heinemann, 2008).
22. See note 1 above, p. 14.
23. See note 1 above, p. 23.

Examining Typical Crimes

2

There are numerous types of crimes that can be experienced by religious institutions. Title 18 of the United States Code outlines federal criminal activity. The statutes can be found at http://www.law.cornell.edu/uscode/text/18.

This chapter focuses on four major classifications of crimes: financial, crimes against property, crimes against people, and hate crimes. Knowing what types of crimes a facility is likely to experience will help you better prepare to prevent or respond to them.

General Crime Information

In order to protect your facility against crime, you need to understand some basic concepts associated with criminal behavior.

Crime Opportunity Model

For a crime to occur, three elements are needed: a motivated offender, a suitable target or victim, and the absence of guardians.[1] When all three elements are present, the criminal has the opportunity to commit a crime. Security seeks to reduce this opportunity, thereby preventing or deterring criminal activity.

Four Elements of a Crime

Basically, a crime has four components: an act, a criminal, a victim, and the location.[2] A crime is any act that is punishable by law. The criminal is the offender, and the victim is who they offend against, whether it is taking their property or assaulting them. Religious institutions can be victims as well as individuals. The goal of security is to keep your institution from being the place where a crime is committed and to prevent your institution from being the victim. The rest of this book will provide tips on how to accomplish that.

Four Stages of Crime

The stages of a crime are surveillance, invitation, confrontation, and assault.[3] Surveillance is when a criminal looks for a potential victim, whether it is an individual or a facility. Invitation refers to the opportunity the victim presents for an attack. For example, if a person stops or slows down when nearing an assailant. An open window, unlocked door, or lack of security measures can be considered a building's "invitation" to crime.

The confrontation is the beginning of the act of the crime itself. It can be forced entry into the building or approaching a victim.[4] Finally, the assault is the crime itself whether it is rape, robbery, or physical assault. It is the crime committed against the individual or facility.

The primary weakness of the assailant occurs at the surveillance stage.[5] This is where you can deter the crime.

Financial Crimes

Many religious institutions receive donations from members during services. In addition, those attending services usually bring their purses and wallets.

Facilities take in money in a variety of ways other than offerings. This includes vending machines, donations, book sales, funding drives, special offerings, mission trips, and collections for those in need.[6] Cash is particularly vulnerable as it is disposable, not traceable, easily assimilated into a thief's possession, and there is no waiting period for use. In addition, to handle the finances of the facility, religious institutions often have credit cards and checking accounts that can be compromised or misappropriated.

Types of Financial Crimes

Financial crimes are often, but not always, committed by insiders who handle the organization's finances. In positions of trust, they often have access to financial instruments. Without proper oversight and procedures, finances may be vulnerable to misappropriation.

Embezzlement

Embezzlement means to willfully "take, or convert to one's own use, another's money or property of which the wrongdoer acquired possession lawfully, by reason of some office or employment, or position of trust."[7] The crime must meet three criteria in order to be considered embezzlement.

1. There must be a relationship between the owner of the money and the defendant.[8]
2. The money must have come into the possession of the defendant by virtue of the relationship.[9]
3. There must be an intentional and fraudulent appropriation or conversion of the money.[10]

This involves using organizational funds for personal use whether it is cash, corporate checks, or company credit cards. The individual has legitimate access to the funds, but uses them for personal enrichment instead of for their allocated and intended purpose. Examples of this include an office manager using checks from the religious institution to pay personal bills or a religious leader using charitable donations for gambling.

There are several ways to prevent this from happening.

1. Keep accurate counts of all funds.
2. Have monthly, quarterly, and annual audits conducted by someone who does not handle the money.
3. Practice separation of duties.
4. Have someone else reconcile the payments and bills.
5. Establish checks and balances.
6. Develop policies and procedures and enforce compliance with them.
7. Have an independent third-party organization conduct audits at least annually.

Separation of duties is a method of internal control in which money handling duties are separated from the record keeping duties. Misappropriation would have to involve two or more dishonest people working together. If only one person handles the money and the record keeping, they can easily steal and falsify the books to conceal the theft.

Skimming

Skimming is taking money before it is recorded on the books. This is difficult to catch as the institution will be unaware that the money was theirs. For example, if someone takes money from a collection plate or donation box before it is counted, no one within the institution would have any idea that funds were missing.

Larceny

Larceny involves taking money that has already been recorded in financial books. This is easier to catch and track because the amount is known. However, if the records are falsified, the theft may not be discovered until an audit is completed.

Fraud and Other Scams

Fraud typically includes benevolence frauds in which an individual seeks assistance by misrepresentation of financial need.[11] A common form is to call a religious institution claiming to be a new member and requesting money for gas, food, or rent that is used instead for drugs, alcohol, or other personal items. Other forms of religious cons include funding "missionary trips" that do not actually occur and false charities.

Affinity Fraud

Affinity fraud occurs when the fraudster uses his/her status as a member of a particular group in order to con members of that group. Individuals immediately trust someone who is "one of us" whether it is a member of the same religious tradition or religious institution.

Scam artists may use lists of members' names and addresses to find additional victims. They may say "The Smiths on Stone Street utilized our services, contributed to our charity, etc." in an attempt to legitimize their operation. This artificially creates trust.

Warning Signs of Potential Fraud Schemes

1. Guaranteed returns, particularly if of a specific percentage such as 10%, regardless of what the market is doing.
2. Advertised as "risk-free."
3. The salesperson (or their firm) is the only one who knows how to invest in it.
4. You must put money down immediately, or you will lose the opportunity forever.
5. Only a "special" group of investors are invited to partake.
6. The investment is an "alternative" to traditional investment practices.

Reducing Vulnerability to Fraud Schemes

Investigate any and all requests for financial assistance, investment opportunities, and offers for sales of products and services. If it sounds too good to be true, it probably is.

Check references of contractors to avoid being victims of repair scams and make sure you have a contract for the work to be performed. In addition, instead of giving them money up front, try to reimburse them for the cost of materials, resources, and other supplies if possible. Ask for bills for labor and hours so the treasurer can pay them. To protect your facility from having liens placed on the property if the contractor does not pay their bills, obtain a notarized *Contractors Affidavit and Waiver of Material Liens* that states "all subcontractors have been paid and that all suppliers have been paid" after the job has been completed.[12]

Some institutions may consider occasionally losing money to scams part of the cost of charitable work. However, it takes money away from those who truly need assistance. In addition, it makes members less inclined to continue donations.

To lessen the chance of need scams, you should set certain rules for distribution of money. Set a specific day and time when you will hear and answer requests, such as every Wednesday at 2 o'clock in the afternoon. This tends to weed out those who truly do not need the money. Legitimate requestors will not have any trouble following the rules. If requested to pay bills, ask for the bill and write the check directly to the company instead of individuals. Give out gas cards or gift cards to grocery stores instead of cash. Require an application to demonstrate financial need. Refer them to other aid organizations including state and federal agencies for assistance.

To guard against investment fraud, use The Ponzi Detection Quiz prior to making any purchase or investing any money.[13] If the proposal scores a single point on the scale, it is very questionable, and the money should be invested in legitimate opportunities instead.

1. Is the investment registered with the SEC or State Securities Division? If NO, score 1 point.
2. Is the sales representative registered with the State Securities Division? If NO, score 1 point.
3. Is the investment being sold as a private placement? If YES, score 1 point.
4. Is the investment a limited partnership? If YES, score 1 point.
5. Does the investment have a 10% commission? If YES, score 1 point.
6. Does the investment have a guaranteed return? If YES, score 1 point.
7. Are you being offered a high rate of return paid by the day, week, or month? If YES, score 1 point.

8. Was the investment being sold as risk-free? If YES, score 1 point.
9. Did the salesperson claim it was an alternative investment? If YES, score 1 point.
10. Was the investment advertised as a retirement plan or 401(k) approved? If YES, score 1 point.

Legitimate investment opportunities do not have these characteristics and are properly registered with the SEC.

Protection from Fraud

1. Practice due diligence.
2. If it sounds too good to be true, it probably is.
3. Donate to established charities only.
4. Verify charities with charitynavigator.org.

If your religious institution has been victimized financially, it is important to admit mistakes as "denial will keep a congregation from examining current policies and finding ways to prevent these types of crimes."[14] Do not allow relationships, bonds, or familiarity to interfere with a police investigation. Prosecute fraudsters and embezzlers regardless of their role in the organization.

Extortion

Extortion is the obtaining of property—including cash—from another induced by use of actual or threatened force, violence, fear, or under color of law – i.e. under the authority of your office.

Although it may seem simplistic, the best way to guard against this type of scheme is to not do anything that could be used against you.

Financial Security Procedures

Do not let one person handle the money. This protects them from false accusations as well as reducing the likelihood that they will take the money.

To maintain security of an institution's finances, there are four key aspects of finances that should be examined[15]:

1. Collections, counting, and deposits
2. Check-writing, expenditures, and accounts access
3. Petty cash
4. Reporting and auditing

A financial security policy should be developed to outline how money should be handled, counted, deposited, reported, and audited.[16] The following sections provide tips on security measures for finances. These procedures should be codified into the financial security policy.

Collections, Counting, and Deposits

1. The room where counting occurs should be secure; preferably with a steel door installed with a peephole and dead bolts.[17]
2. Have at least two people – a guardian and a lookout – outside the door.[18]
3. The counting room should have a telephone and a silent duress alarm.[19]
4. At least two people should collect and take contributions to the counting space.
5. At least two members of a counting team should be present at all times during counting.
6. A minimum of two unrelated people should count the collections, and they should be rotated frequently.
7. Collections should be counted twice—once by each member of the counting team.
8. Never allow a member to take funds home for any reason.
9. Cash should be placed in a sealed envelope with the total written on the outside of the envelope.[20]
10. Funds should immediately be taken to a secure location or to a bank by at least two individuals.
11. Funds should be transported in a locked container.
12. A second copy of the deposit slip should be given to the administrator, pastor, treasurer, or another person who had nothing to do with the counting of funds.[21]
13. Funds placed in the bank must be independently verified against the counting team deposit slip.[22]
14. Offering envelopes and a copy of the deposit slip should be given to a person who is responsible for recording the individual giving from the membership.[23]
15. Funds received during the week should be receipted by at least two accountable individuals.[24]

Checks, Credit Cards, and Expenditures

1. Lock credit cards and checks in a safe along with cash.[25]
2. Use a purchase order system to request and obligate expenditures from funds.[26]
3. Checks should be dated appropriately and immediately endorsed.[27]

Petty Cash

1. Keep petty cash in a secure location that is not the secretary's desk, which is too common a hiding place.[28]
2. Balance the box at regular intervals.
3. One person should have the duty of dispensing money and keeping accurate records.
4. Establish policies for permissible uses and the maximum that can be withdrawn at one time.
5. Consider asking staff to make minor purchases and to bring in receipts for reimbursement.[29]
6. Limit the number of people who know where the box is kept.

Reporting and Auditing

1. Monitor the books.
2. Have a periodic outside independent auditor of books.
3. Regardless of accounting methods used, funds should be posted so an accurate depiction of funds available, funds obligated, and funds expended are provided.[30]
4. There should be a balance sheet system to reconcile funds received, funds obligated, materials or resources received, and payments made.[31]
5. Have, at a minimum, a monthly statement of the accounts reported to the facility.[32]

Other Financial Management Techniques

To make the institution a less attractive target, signage associated with financial management can be posted such as the following[33]:

1. Deposits are not kept overnight.
2. Records only—no cash.
3. We do not keep money in this safe.

Crimes against Property

In these crimes, the primary target is tangible property. In some cases, like arson, people can be hurt, but they are not the primary target.

Types of Property Crimes

Arson

Arson has become such a prevalent attack method on churches that in 1996 Congress established the Church Arson Prevention Act.[34] In fact, the leading cause of fire at worship facilities in the United States is arson.[35] Between 1995 and 2000, over 1500 houses of worship were damaged by fire or bombing, including 900 arson fires.[36] Motives include pyromania, vandalism, covering up other crimes, financial profit, retaliation, and hate crimes.[37]

Religious institutions are particularly vulnerable due to long periods of vacancy. The National Church Arson Task Force recommends the following measures to reduce vulnerability to arson[38]:

1. Cut shrubbery and trees to provide visibility.
2. Do not allow signs to block the view of the building.
3. Secure ladders and stairways that provide roof access.
4. Consider decorative or wrought iron protection for windows.
5. Install floodlights on the exterior of the building.

Arson prevention is also accidental fire prevention. The measures that can prevent or mitigate damage caused by accident can do the same for fires caused intentionally. These include the following:

1. Use fire-resistant and fire-retardant carpets, draperies, and other materials.
2. Install good outside lighting.
3. Secure doors and windows.
4. Install a sprinkler system.
5. Install a smoke and/or heat detector.
6. Program lights to come on automatically and at random intervals.
7. Install motion detector lights at outside entrances.
8. Conduct periodic fire drills.
9. Discourage smoking within or near the exterior of the structure.
10. Store combustible materials in a safe place.
11. Never leave lights or candles on overnight or while unattended.

Bombing

Bombs can be constructed to look harmless and delivered or placed in a variety of ways. Backpacks, coolers, and packages are some of the methods for delivering explosives. Procedures for handling suspicious mail, objects, or packages can be found in Chapter 9 "Reacting to an Event in Progress." Bomb threats are also covered in that chapter. The most important countermeasures are to refrain from touching the object, isolate the suspected object, evacuate the immediate area, open windows to assist in venting potentially explosive gases, and contact law enforcement.[39]

Vandalism

Vandalism is not just graffiti. It can cause extensive property damage as well as incite fear in employees and attendees. Examples include graffiti; broken windows; paint thrown on statuary, doors, or steps; removal of landscaping elements such as flowers or trees; destruction of playground equipment; egging of the facility; and leaving dead animals on the grounds.

Acts of vandalism are not for monetary profit, but they are often symbolic attacks. Although teenagers are frequently accused, vandalism has become a tool of racial hatred, religious prejudice, and radical activism as well.[40] It can be a symbolic attack against a particular stance of the individual religious institution or against the religious tradition of which they are members.

In addition, there are instances of social prejudice wherein a facility is attacked due to the notoriety of a member who may have committed a crime, as evidenced by an attack on the Catholic Church attended by John Demjanjuk after he was convicted of Nazi war crimes.[41] The entire organization suffered due to the acts of one individual, even though his actions were not reflective of the institution's beliefs.

Vandalism often occurs indoors as perpetrators can carry out more destruction where there is less chance of being observed. In some cases, it can conceal another crime that has been thwarted, such as burglary, either because there is nothing of value or because there are locks or other measures that prevent them from reaching their target.[42]

Theft and Burglary

Many churches possess physical assets that are likely to be attractive targets. These can include sound equipment, office equipment, and audiovisual equipment. In addition, some have altar decorations and icons that are made of precious metals. Some churches have valuable artwork and other items that may tempt burglars.

Security Measures for Property

Engraving valuables with identifying numbers or other marks can help locate stolen property quickly. An inventory system with pictures will make it easier for law enforcement to recover your property. Insuring them will also enable you to recoup some financial costs if the property cannot be recovered or is damaged beyond repair due to arson or vandalism.

In addition to these measures, physical security measures such as safes; locks on doors and file cabinets; adequate lighting of doors, windows, and parking lots; and alarm systems will help safeguard property. Physical security procedures and equipment protect the building and property of the religious institution from crimes such as theft, vandalism, and arson. Chapter 5 will discuss these elements in more detail.

Crimes against Persons

Crimes against persons are committed against those who work at or attend your facility. They can be targeted victims or simply victims of opportunity.

Types of Crimes against Persons

Crimes in this category include the following:

1. Robbery
2. Harassment/stalking
3. Assault and battery
4. Sexual assault
5. Homicide

Robbery

Robbery is similar to theft, but involves taking money directly from the victim's person. Armed or unarmed, the robber uses intimidation and the threat of force or fear to deprive victims of their cash and material goods.

What to Do during a Robbery
1. Remain calm.
2. Cooperate.
3. Do what you are told.
4. Help the robber get in and out as quickly as possible.[43]
5. Don't speak unless told to.
6. Don't debate or argue.
7. Don't do anything you are not ordered to do.
8. Keep your hands open and in plain view.[44]
9. Remember: Lives are more important than money or property.

Assault, Sexual Assault, and Homicide

These crimes involve physical contact with the victim. As a result, prevention and response will be similar.

1. Do not allow anyone to be alone within the facility or on the grounds.
2. Establish access control procedures.
3. Make sure rooms have telephones.

4. Educate attendees on identifying suspicious behavior.
5. Trust your instincts.
6. Call security or law enforcement.

Personal Security Measures

First and foremost, no individual should be alone in the facility. This makes them vulnerable to attack. Establish policies and procedures on meeting with announced visitors, screening of employees and volunteers, and dealing with suspicious individuals.

Additional security measures can be found in Chapter 5 on choosing physical and electronic security countermeasures, Chapter 8 on identifying and handling at-risk individuals, Chapter 14 on increasing security awareness, and Chapter 19 on protecting children and youth.

Hate Crimes

Hate crimes can be any of the previously described crimes, but they are frequently arson, assault, vandalism, and bombings. The difference, however, is in the motive. In a hate crime, the primary motive is hatred of a characteristic of the victim such as their religious or ethnic background.

The FBI's 2012 Hate Crime Statistics reveal the following information of the 1340 victims of an antireligious hate crime[45]:

- 62.4% were victims of anti-Jewish bias.
- 11.6% were victims of anti-Islamic bias.
- 7.5% were victims of a bias against groups of individuals of varying religions (anti-multiple religions, group).
- 6.4% were victims of an anti-Catholic bias.
- 2.6% were victims of an anti-Protestant bias.
- 0.9% were victims of an anti-Atheist/Agnostic bias.
- 8.6% were victims of a bias against other religions (anti-other religion).

The Southern Poverty Law Center also tracks hate crimes. These are just a few of the hate crime incidents against religious institutions they have compiled from 2009 to 2014.[46]

- 2014
  - Orland Park, IL: A bullet was fired through the dome of a mosque during a prayer service.
- 2013
  - Memphis, TN: A security guard pleaded guilty to violating the civil rights of students of a Jewish school by defacing the school's Torah scroll and prayer books before a January 2013 worship service.
  - Miami Beach, FL: The letters "KKK" and a bull's eye were spray-painted on a mikvah—a ritual bathhouse for Jewish women—as well as on a youth center, a condominium, and a homeless outreach center.

- Fargo, ND: A man was arraigned on two counts of transmitting threatening communications and one count of interference with a federally protected activity for allegedly calling a synagogue in January 2011 and leaving a threatening message he claimed was from Hamas.
- Westport, MA: A church was vandalized, and its tabernacle was stolen.
- Fort Lauderdale, FL: Swastikas were spray-painted inside a church that operates a day care center. The building was then set on fire.
- Wilmington, MA: The word "brainwashing" was spray-painted on the outside of three churches.
- Land O'Lakes, FL: A man was allegedly shot in the face with a pellet gun by another man who asked if the victim was Muslim.
- Bangor, ME: Three teens were arrested for spray-painting swastikas and anti-Semitic graffiti on two synagogues on September 21.
- 2012
  - Buffalo, MN: A man was charged with felony vandalism for allegedly throwing rocks and leaving anti-gay posters at four churches.
  - Bay Shore, NY: Anti-Muslim epithets were spray-painted on a mosque.
  - Harrisburg, VA: Racial and ethnic slurs and sexually explicit images were spray-painted on an Islamic center.
  - Staten Island, NY: Packages of uncooked bacon were strewn around a park where hundreds of Muslims were celebrating Ramadan.
  - Coral Springs, FL: A swastika and two pentagrams were painted on a bus belonging to a synagogue.
  - Joplin, MO: A mosque was set on fire.
  - Hayward, CA: Four teens, ages 13 to 16, were arrested on suspicion of defacing property and a hate crime for allegedly throwing lemons at a local mosque, striking at least one person.
  - Belleville, IL: An 18-year-old man was charged with one count of burglary, one count of criminal damage to property, and one count of hate crime after he allegedly vandalized a church and wrote a racial epithet inside.
  - Crawfordville, FL: A swastika and racist symbols and remarks were painted inside a church that was vandalized.
  - Arkana, AR: The words "White Power," the letters "KKK," and antireligious graffiti were spray-painted inside a church.
  - Waymart, PA: Five people allegedly yelled racial epithets, destroyed property, and shot paintballs at campers at a Jewish summer camp several times in July.
  - Murfreesboro, TN: A man was charged with interfering with the religious freedom of members of a mosque by threatening to use force against them when he allegedly left a racist message threatening to bomb the building in 2011. The man was also charged with threatening to use an explosive device to interfere with religious freedom.
  - Brooklyn, NY: Swastikas were spray-painted on a synagogue, two businesses, a building, and two vehicles in an Orthodox Jewish neighborhood.
  - Glendale, AZ: Satanic symbols and antireligious graffiti were spray-painted on a Catholic church.
  - Jurupa Valley, CA: Two 18-year-olds and two teens were charged with burglary, committing a hate crime, and conspiracy for allegedly vandalizing a Mormon church.
  - Philadelphia, PA: Dozens of BBs were fired at a synagogue while more than a hundred people were attending an event there.

- Blue Point, NY: Antireligious graffiti, including "666," was written on a sign at a Catholic church.
- Santa Cruz, CA: Graffiti that included antireligious messages was spray-painted on a Catholic church that was vandalized.
- Chantilly, VA: A young man was charged with felony destruction of property for allegedly vandalizing a mosque that was under construction in January.
- Chicago, IL: Anti-Semitic remarks were spray-painted on a local synagogue.
- Bushnell, FL: Jewish headstones in a veterans' cemetery were vandalized.
- Hackensack, NJ: A young man was arrested in connection with the January 3 firebombing of a synagogue in Paramus and the January 11 firebombing of a synagogue in Rutherford. He was also accused of spray-painting anti-Semitic and white supremacist graffiti at two temples in December.
- Sterling Heights, MI: Hate graffiti was scrawled on a Sikh place of worship.
- Golden City, MO: A racial slur directed at Latinos was written on a church window.
- Chantilly, VA: A mosque was vandalized.
- Springfield, IL: A man was sentenced to 4.5 years in prison after pleading guilty to felony charges of conspiracy to violate civil rights, religious property damage because of race, and damage to religious property by use of fire for his part in burning a black church after the 2008 presidential election.
- Temecula, CA: A bench with a pentagram scrawled on it was tossed into a fountain outside a Catholic church, and then a charred Bible was left outside the church's main doors.
- Elmont, NY: A man was charged with one count of arson as a hate crime, four counts of arson, and five counts of criminal possession of a weapon for allegedly firebombing a convenience store, two residences in Queens, a home in Nassau County, and an Islamic center on New Year's Day.
- 2011
  - Yonkers, NY: Four statues of the Virgin Mary in shrines or Nativity scenes in the yards of residences were painted black. A statue of the Virgin was stolen from outside a church, and several statues inside were painted black.
  - Midland, TX: A man was sentenced to more than 37 years in prison after pleading guilty to charges of damaging religious property, arson, and interfering with housing, all prosecuted with a bias crime enhancement, for firebombing a black church in the city of Crane in December 2010.
  - San Jose, CA: A Hindu man, whose family is originally from India, was allegedly beaten by a group of men who called him a "terrorist."
  - New Orleans, LA: Antireligious slurs such as "Heil Mary" were written on prayer cards at an Episcopal church. An angel statue was also vandalized, and an Aryan Nations symbol was written on it.
  - Ansonville, NC: Swastikas, racial slurs, and other graffiti were spray-painted on the exterior of seven churches, and the interior of one of the churches was vandalized.
  - Milpitas, CA: Pentagrams and vulgarities were spray-painted on a Lutheran church.
  - Wichita, KS: A mosque that had been receiving anti-Muslim letters for months was set on fire.
  - Michigan City, IN: Rocks and a large cinder block were thrown through the window of an Islamic center.
  - Cherry Hill, NJ: The hands on a statue of Mary at St. Mary's Church were broken off.
  - Mount Dora, FL: A new synagogue was spray-painted with anti-Semitic graffiti.
  - Danville, VA: Swastikas were painted on the door and sidewalk of a synagogue.

- ◦ Sapulpa, OK: A burned cross was left on the lawn of a black church.
- ◦ Portland, ME: Anti-Islamic graffiti was painted on the city's largest mosque following the death of Osama bin Laden.
- ◦ Stockton, CA: A mosque was set on fire.
- ◦ Wisconsin Dells, WI: Two swastikas were spray-painted on a Native American church.
- ◦ Fort Worth, TX: A man was indicted for vandalizing a mosque.
- ◦ Hollywood, CA: A church's sign supporting marriage equality was vandalized.
- ◦ Anaheim, CA: Antireligious graffiti was painted on a church.
- ◦ Waterbury, CT: A large swastika was spray-painted on a synagogue.
- ◦ Manhattan, NY: An Upper West Side synagogue received a bomb threat in the mail.
- • 2010
  - ◦ Columbia, SC: An Islamic center in South Carolina was defaced with bacon strips.
  - ◦ Carlton, NY: Five teenagers drove in front of the World Sufi Foundation mosque while honking car horns and yelling obscenities during a religious service.
  - ◦ Mobile, AL: A man pleaded guilty to vandalizing a local Messianic Jewish house of worship and having the makings of a homemade bomb.
  - ◦ Oak Park, CA: "Get out of Oak Park" was painted on a synagogue.
  - ◦ Wilmington, DE: "Go home" was spray painted on the Korean United Methodist Church.
  - ◦ Olney, MD: Swastikas, "Kill Jews," and the words "Arbeit Macht Frei"—the same phrase that was painted above the entrance to Auschwitz concentration camp meaning "work will set you free"—were spray painted on a synagogue.
  - ◦ Bellevue, WA: A van parked near a mosque and bearing advertisements about Islam was smeared with what appeared to be dog feces.
  - ◦ Los Angeles, CA: The numerals "666" were scrawled in the kitchen of a Catholic church, a knife was stuck into a religious painting, and feces were left in the church's auditorium.
  - ◦ Jacksonville, FL: A homemade pipe bomb exploded at an Islamic center.
  - ◦ Idaho Falls, ID: Rocks with derogatory messages about Mormons were thrown through windows at a Church of Jesus Christ of Latter-day Saints.
  - ◦ Collinsville, IL: An upside-down cross, the numerals "666," and a picture of the male anatomy were spray-painted on the side of a church.
  - ◦ Mt. Sinai, NY: Motor oil was poured onto an entrance of the Kingdom Hall of Jehovah's Witnesses.
  - ◦ Tarzana, CA: Police investigate a hate crime at a Lutheran church.
  - ◦ Oakland, CA: The Greek Orthodox Cathedral of the Ascension was vandalized with racist graffiti.
  - ◦ Norfolk, VA: A man pleaded guilty to pasting stickers depicting anti-Semitic, anti-gay, and racist messages on four synagogues.
  - ◦ Boca Raton, FL: A Jewish temple was vandalized with racist graffiti.
  - ◦ Nashville, TN: "Muslims go home" was spray-painted on a mosque.
- • 2009
  - ◦ Seattle, WA: A jury declared a man guilty of murder in his second trial for the 2006 shooting spree at a Seattle Jewish center.

Other organizations track hate crimes against members of their own religion as well. Real Sikhism tracks hate crimes against Sikhs at www.realsikhism.com/index. php?subaction=showfull&id=1192337092&ucat=8.

Hate Crime Security Measures

Since hate crimes often involve assault, vandalism, bombing, or arson, the security measures that are meant to counter these activities work regardless of the adversary's motives. These include physical and electronic security measures such as alarm systems and CCTV. However, it is important to take threats seriously, particularly if they seem to be targeting your facility due to the religious tradition.

Final Thoughts

Fortunately, measures that protect against one type of crime also protect against other types of crime. The following general rules for security measures will help protect against most threats.

General Rules—Interior

1. Never meet alone with unannounced strangers.
2. Be wary of the following:
   a. those who want to be alone in the sanctuary,[47]
   b. those who want to take a tour of the facility,[48]
   c. those who enter during services,
   d. and those who want cash or a check made out to them to "pay bills."
3. Secure the interior.
4. Lock all exterior doors and windows.
5. Keep doors, closets, storage units, and cabinets locked.
6. Maintain key control.
7. Install an alarm system.
8. Do not store paint or other items that can be used to vandalize.

General Rules—Exterior

1. Have a definable perimeter with walls, fences, or hedges.
2. Have good exterior lighting.
3. Limit access to the back of the building.
4. Limit access to groundskeeper tools.[49]
5. Limit parking lot access after-hours.
6. Ask local law enforcement to drive through the parking lot when there are no activities.
7. Use "anti-climb" paint on gutters and drains to prevent climbing. It should be at least 8-ft high.[50] It never dries and is very slippery.
8. Use unbreakable glazing or polycarbonate sheets over stained glass windows.[51]
9. Install motion detector lights on exterior doorways and near parking lots.

Crime can be prevented in your facility. Knowing the types of crimes common in your area as well as identifying threats can help you design an effective security plan for protecting your facility. Chapter 4 will show you how to evaluate the risks inherent to your particular facility so you can ensure the countermeasures you select will be most applicable to your situation. Before we do that, however, we will discuss basic security principles in Chapter 3.

End Notes

1. Quarles C. L. and Ratliff P. L., *Crime Prevention for Houses of Worship* (Alexandria: American Society for Industrial Security, 2001).
2. Ibid.
3. Ibid.
4. Ibid.
5. Ibid.
6. American Crime Prevention Institute, *Church Crime Prevention* (2008). Retrieved from http://www.santarosa.fl.gov/coad/documents/ChurchCrimePreventionVSept2008.pdf.
7. Wells J. T., *Corporate Fraud Handbook*, Third Edition (Hoboken: John Wiley & Sons, 2011), 3.
8. Wells J. T., *Corporate Fraud Handbook*, Third Edition (Hoboken: John Wiley & Sons, 2011).
9. Ibid.
10. Ibid.
11. See note 6 above.
12. See note 1 above, p. 83.
13. Hamilton P. R., *Ponzi Schemes and Investment Fraud* (Charleston: CreateSpace, 2012).
14. See note 1 above, p. 80.
15. Hanna J. W., *Safe and Secure: The Alban Guide to Protecting Your Congregation* (Herndon: Alban Institute, 1999).
16. See note 6 above.
17. See note 1 above.
18. See note 1 above.
19. See note 1 above.
20. Welch R. H., *Serving by Safeguarding Your Church* (Grand Rapids: Zondervan Press, 2002).
21. Ibid.
22. Ibid.
23. Ibid.
24. Ibid.
25. See note 1 above.
26. See note 20 above.
27. See note 20 above.
28. Hanna J. W., *Safe and Secure: The Alban Guide to Protecting Your Congregation* (Alban Institute, 1999).
29. Ibid.
30. See note 20 above.
31. See note 20 above.
32. See note 20 above.
33. See note 1 above.
34. See note 1 above.
35. National Church Arson Task Force, *Threat Assessment Guide for Houses of Worship* (2000) Retrieved from http://www.scnus.org/local_includes/downloads/9186.pdf.
36. Ibid.
37. Ibid.
38. Ibid.
39. Ibid.
40. See note 1 above.

41. See note 1 above.
42. See note 1 above.
43. See note 1 above, p. 96.
44. See note 1 above.
45. http://www.fbi.gov/about-us/cjis/ucr/hate-crime/2012/topic-pages/victims/victims_final.
46. http://www.splcenter.org/get-informed/hate-incidents.
47. See note 1 above.
48. See note 1 above.
49. See note 1 above.
50. See note 1 above.
51. See note 1 above.

Understanding Basic Security Principles

This chapter focuses on basic security principles and concepts and shows you how to apply them to your facility. We will revisit these concepts throughout the rest of the book.

"Security provides those means, active or passive, which serve to protect and preserve an environment that allows for the conduct of activities within the organization or society without disruption."[1] It is "an integrated system of activities, systems, programs, facilities, and policies for the protection of organizational information, government information (classified and sensitive unclassified) if appropriate, government and organizational facilities, personnel, property, and equipment."[2]

Security involves many tasks such as the following:

1. Planning
2. Preparedness
3. Access control
4. Crime prevention
5. Crisis management
6. Incident response
7. Security awareness
8. Deterrence
9. Recovery
10. Investigation

Security can be divided into five major areas:

1. Physical
2. Electronic
3. Environmental
4. Operational
5. Information security

Physical security refers to physical elements such as barriers, fences, and locks that secure a site and the people and property within. Electronic security refers to systems such as intrusion detection, alarms, access control, and CCTV. There is considerable overlap with physical security. However, these systems require electricity, which is why they merit their own category.

Environmental security, more commonly referred to as crime prevention through environmental design (CPTED) or crime prevention through opportunity reduction, concerns the use of space to deter potential adversaries. It will be discussed on its own in Chapter 5.

Operational security is concerned with policies and procedures that increase the security of a facility. It focuses on activities and how they are performed. Chapter 7 focuses on developing policies and procedures.

Last is information security. As the majority of information security is operational, it will also be discussed in greater detail in Chapter 7.

General Concepts

This section describes terms that relate to security as a whole. These terms and concepts typically relate to more than one category of security. In addition, they also refer to the interaction between different types of security systems.

Design Basis Threat

This concept stipulates that a physical protection system should be designed based on the maximum credible threat to the facility.[3] What this means is that a system that protects against the most likely threat will also protect against other less likely threats. Therefore, putting your resources toward protecting against the most likely threats will be the most cost-effective. If there is no threat of an aerial attack, then it would be useless to install antiaircraft guns on the roof of your building and a waste of resources, time, and effort.

Protection in Depth

This means that an adversary has to sequentially overcome a number of protection devices in order to accomplish his/her goal.[4] In other words, you have more than one method of protection that an adversary must avoid or defeat in order to cause harm to your facility. For example, there may be a fence around the property, locks on the doors, and intrusion detection systems in case the door is forced open. As a result, the adversary has to scale the fence, force the door open, and disable the alarm in order to commit an act against the facility.

The purpose of this is to negatively affect the adversary. This can affect them in several ways[5]:

1. Increases uncertainty about the system
2. Requires more preparation prior to attacking the system
3. Creates additional steps where the adversary may fail or abort their attempt
4. Provides additional opportunities for detection and response

Minimum Consequence of Component Failure

It is unlikely that a system will not experience some component failure during its lifecycle. Component failures have numerous causes from environmental factors to adversary actions that are beyond the scope of the system's design.[6] Faulty system components or improper connections can also cause failures.

As a result, it is important to have automatic contingency plans that enable the system to continue to operate. Redundant equipment that takes over the function of disabled equipment, such as a generator, is needed.[7] The purpose is to minimize the consequences of component failure to ensure that the system still protects the facility even if a part of it is not working.

Balanced Protection

Balanced protection refers to the idea that "no matter how an adversary attempts to accomplish the goal, effective elements of the PPS [physical protection system] will be encountered."[8] In a balanced system, the minimum time to penetrate each barrier is the same, and the minimum probability of detecting the penetration should be equal as well.[9]

Complete balance is unlikely and undesirable as there is no advantage to over-designing a system.[10] Doors may be adequate as they are, and walls are thick due to safety and structural requirements rather than protection requirements.[11] The ultimate objective is "to provide adequate protection against all threats on all possible paths and to maintain a balance with other considerations, such as cost, safety, or structural integrity."[12] Security should also be balanced with the mission and culture of the organization.

Countermeasures

Countermeasures are procedures, technologies, or physical items that are used to reduce or eliminate vulnerabilities. They are typically divided into three categories: preventive, corrective, and detective.

Preventive measures reduce the likelihood of a deliberate attack, introduce delays, reduce vulnerabilities, or otherwise cause an attack to be unsuccessful. They include both physical and psychological deterrents.[13] They are typically divided into four categories: facility, employees, protective force, and visitor controls.[14]

Corrective measures reduce the effects of an attack and restore the facility to normal operation.[15] They include instructions for monitoring the PPS, assessing the alarms, evaluating information provided by all subsystems, and dispatching an appropriate response.[16] Scenario-based procedures for responding to security breaches are another example.

Detective measures help discover attacks and activate appropriate preventive or corrective measures. Detective countermeasures include the following: display and assessment; intrusion detection; identification; access control; CCTV; communications and search equipment; and investigation.[17]

Access Control

Access control refers to allowing authorized personnel entry into the facility and denying the entry of unauthorized personnel.[18] What this means for a religious institution is that the unauthorized personnel are anyone who would participate in criminal activity.

Throughput or the number of authorized personnel allowed access per unit of time is one of the measures of entry control effectiveness.[19] Unauthorized persons must be prevented from entering and documents/items/information must be prevented from leaving without proper authorization.[20]

Two other measures of effectiveness are false acceptance and false rejection. False acceptance rate is the percentage of unauthorized users who are allowed access to a facility.[21] False reject rate is the opposite of false acceptance in that legitimate users are denied access.[22] You want to reduce both of these rates as much as possible.

Target Hardening

Target hardening is a concept that involves making your facility a less attractive target. This can be accomplished in a multitude of ways such as improved exterior lighting, locks on doors, alarm systems on doors and windows, signage, and cameras.[23] The goal is to eliminate the opportunity for attack and send the message that the risks outweigh the potential rewards for criminals.[24]

Disaster/Crisis/Incident Management Cycle

There are four phases of the disaster cycle: mitigation, preparedness, response, and recovery. Interlinked and interdependent, they are considered a cycle and not a linear or chronological series of steps (Figure 3.1).

The mitigation and preparedness phases occur in anticipation of an event, whereas the response and recovery phases occur during and after the event.[25] These phases can be repeated as necessary for each hazard that occurs. This is important because many hazards often lead to additional disasters. For example,

Figure 3.1 Incident Management Cycle.

a hurricane may cause damaging winds or downed power lines that may cause fires, flooding, or landslides.

Mitigation

Mitigation involves any actions taken to permanently remove or reduce the risk of hazards to human life, property, and function.[26] It is a "sustained action to reduce or eliminate risk to people and property from hazards and their effects."[27] Mitigation is different from the other phases in that it focuses on longterm goals instead of the immediate handling of a disaster and the subsequent recovery.[28] Mitigation activities typically fall under four basic categories.

1. Deterrent controls "reduce the likelihood of a deliberate attack and/or dissuade would-be attackers by making a facility less desirable as a target."[29]
2. Preventive controls "protect vulnerabilities by making an attack unsuccessful or reducing its impact."[30]
3. Corrective controls "reduce the effect of an attack."
4. Detective controls "discover attacks and may trigger preventative or corrective controls."[31]

Preparedness

Preparedness involves actions taken to reduce the impact of forecasted or imminent disasters. Security measures are vital to this stage, and it involves execution of the plans created in the mitigation phase.[32] Preparedness is a state of readiness to respond to any situation that may arise.[33] It involves an ongoing process of assessment, planning, preparation, and evaluation in order to constantly assess the readiness of an area to respond to events.[34]

Response

Response is typically what most people think of when they think of incident management. Response is the set of actions taken during the initial impact of the crisis and its immediate aftermath.[35] It involves first responders, law enforcement, private security, medical professionals, fire professionals, and anyone else who may be called upon to help in an emergency. With its main emphasis on lifesaving and neutralizing the threat, there is some attempt to mitigate damages. However, the main focus is on what is happening at that moment.

Recovery

Once the immediate needs of the community are taken care of, longterm recovery plans are put into action. These may involve reconstruction, cleanup, and other restoration activities. Communities also need to deal with fear and loss of security as well as handling the economic impacts. As a result, psychological recovery must be considered along with physical recovery.

Physical Security

Physical security refers to physical elements such as barriers, fences, and locks that secure a site and the people and property within. Chapter 5 explains several physical security measures that can be applied to your facility.

Electronic Security

As previously stated, electronic security refers to physical systems that require electricity to operate such as intrusion detection, alarms, access control technologies, and CCTV. Chapter 5 will go into more detail on methods of electronic security.

Continuous Line of Detection

This concept applies to sensors and ensures that there are no breaks in the detection field. Uniform detection around the perimeter is a design goal of the PPS system. Sensors should be configured so that detection zones overlap.[36] Any gaps in detection could be where adversaries enter the perimeter undetected.

Environmental Security

An urban planning and design process, it is a comprehensive approach combining traditional crime prevention techniques with newly developed theories and methods.[37] This concept is particularly important for religious institutions as its goal is to reduce criminal opportunities and the fear of crime without resorting to making the facility look like a maximum security prison.[38] Chapter 6 explains how you can use these principles to secure your facility. It also known as crime prevention through environmental design (CPTED).

Operational Security

Operational security involves "how" things are done. It includes the following elements[39]:

1. Organization and staffing
2. Policies and procedures
3. Training
4. Visitor control
5. Security guard staffing
6. Post order assignment and execution
7. Alarm and incident assessment
8. Incident responses
9. Administration of security systems

10. Delivery processing
11. Emergency response

Information Security

Information of some kind is a key element of anything and everything an organization does. There are three major core components of information security that must be taken into account.[40]

1. People
2. Processes
3. Technology

Information security based on people involves hiring the proper staff and the right number of individuals. It also concerns volunteers and who has access to what. Process refers to policies, standards, and procedures that are well-written, consistently enforced, and constantly evaluated and updated.[41] Technology involves protecting information with authentication and authorization; firewalls and virtual private networks; antivirus software; intrusion detection; content filtering; and encryption.

Information security threats fall into several main categories.[42]

1. Acts of human error or failure
2. Compromises to intellectual property
3. Deliberate acts of espionage or trespass
4. Deliberate acts of information extortion
5. Deliberate acts of theft
6. Deliberate software attacks
7. Deviations in quality of service from service providers
8. Forces of nature
9. Technical hardware failures or errors
10. Technical software failures or errors
11. Technological obsolescence

Most information security threats are from one of two categories: general attacks and targeted attacks.[43] General attacks are phishing or mail spoofing in which hundreds of emails are sent out in the hopes that at least one will be answered. Targeted attacks are specifically focused on your organization or individuals within it. Both can present a significant threat. Education and vigilance are the most effective countermeasures against these threats.[44]

Acts of human error and failure are difficult to guard against. Everyone makes mistakes at some point. Natural disasters can also be unpredictable and difficult to fully protect against. Having the most current hardware and software, as well as a competent IT department can help guard against technological obsolescence as well as technical software and hardware failures or errors. Therefore, most information security strategies seek to guard against deliberate attacks and inadvertent compromise of sensitive information.

To be comprehensive, information security must address the following key concepts.[45]

Key Concepts of Information Security

1. Confidentiality
2. Integrity
3. Availability
4. Privacy
5. Identification
6. Authentication
7. Authorization
8. Accountability

The three primary concepts are what are often called the CIA Triad or Triangle.[46] The three elements of the triangle are confidentiality, integrity, and availability.

Confidentiality

Confidentiality means that information is disseminated only to those with sufficient privileges and a demonstrated need to have access to such information. A component of privacy, it is meant to protect information from unauthorized viewing.[47] Confidentiality is compromised by interception attacks in which unauthorized persons access information such as eavesdropping, stealing laptops, reading over someone's shoulder, sending emails to the wrong person, or unauthorized copying of files.[48] These attacks can be very difficult to detect.

Integrity

Integrity means that data is uncorrupted and undamaged. It is "the ability to prevent our data from being changed in an unauthorized or undesirable manner."[49] Protecting the integrity of data involves setting user permissions as well as features that let you undo undesirable changes.[50]

Integrity can be compromised by interruption, modification, and fabrication. Interruption means assets become unusable or unavailable on a temporary or permanent basis.[51] Modification involves making changes or tampering with information assets. Fabrication involves generating suspicious information in the form of data, processes, communications, or other activities within a system.[52]

Availability

Availability refers to the ability of users to access information without obstruction or interference. Availability can be compromised by power outages, problems with applications or operating systems, network connectivity issues, denial of service attacks, and compromise of systems.[53] Like integrity, availability can be compromised by interruption, modification, and fabrication.

In addition to the CIA Triad, there are additional concepts that are important to information security.

Privacy

Privacy means that information will only be used in ways fully disclosed and accepted by those providing it.

Identification

Identification is the foundation of subsequent authentication and authorization. It is an assertion that you are who you claim to be.[54] Methods of identification can be falsified or the information can be compromised and used fraudulently.

Authentication

Authentication requires proving that a user is who they claim they are. Usernames and associated passwords are a method of authentication. To put it simply, it is the set of methods used to establish the veracity of an identity claim.[55]

Authorization

Authorization verifies that the user has permission to access, update, delete, or otherwise alter the contents of an information asset. It is closely tied to access control, which enables access to be managed at a very basic level.[56]

Accountability

Accountability is the assurance that every action can be attributed to a named person or automated process. It provides the means to trace activities back to their source.[57] This can be crucial to investigations of suspicious activity.

Final Thoughts

Now that you understand the basic security principles, you can apply them to protecting your facility. But before you can properly secure your facility, you need to evaluate the risks associated with it. The next chapter will show you how to identify the most likely risks to your facility so you can design a security program to effectively protect your facility.

End Notes

1. Quarles C. L. and Ratliff P., *Crime Prevention for Houses of Worship* (Alexandria: ASIS, 2001), 5.
2. Roper C., *Risk Management for Security Professionals* (Massachusetts: Butterworth-Heinemann, 1999), 4.
3. Garcia M. L., *The Design and Evaluation of Physical Protection Systems*, Second Edition (Massachusetts: Butterworth-Heinemann, 2008).

4. Ibid.

5. Ibid.

6. Garcia M. L., *The Design and Evaluation of Physical Protection Systems*, Second Edition (Boston: Butterworth-Heinemann, 2008).

7. Ibid.

8. Ibid, p. 59.

9. Ibid.

10. Ibid.

11. Ibid.

12. Ibid, p. 60.

13. Patterson D. G., *Implementing Physical Protection Systems: A Practical Guide* (Alexandria: ASIS International, 2004).

14. Ibid.

15. Ibid.

16. Ibid.

17. Ibid.

18. See note 6 above.

19. See note 6 above.

20. Fennelly L. J., *Effective Physical Security*, Third Edition (Boston: Butterworth-Heinemann, 2004).

21. Whitman M. E. and Mattord H. J., *Management of Information Security*, Second Edition (Boston: Thomson Course Technology, 2010).

22. Ibid.

23. American Crime Prevention Institute, *Church Crime Prevention* (2008). Retrieved from http://www.santarosa.fl.gov/coad/documents/ChurchCrimePreventionVSept2008.pdf.

24. Ibid.

25. www.gdrc.org/uem/disasters/1-dm_cycle.html .

26. McGlown K. J., *Terrorism and Disaster Management: Preparing Healthcare Leaders for the New Reality* (Chicago: Health Administration Press, 2004).

27. Haddow G. D., Bullock J. A. and Coppola D. P., *Introduction to Emergency Management*, Fourth Edition (Boston: Butterworth-Heinemann, 2011), p. 57.

28. Haddow G. D., Bullock J. A. and Coppola D. P., *Introduction to Emergency Management*, Fourth Edition (Boston: Butterworth-Heinemann, 2011).

29. See note 26 above, p. 56.

30. See note 26 above, p. 56.

31. See note 26 above, p. 56.

32. Alexander D., *Principles of Emergency Planning and Management* (New York: Oxford University Press, 2002).

33. Haddow G. D., Bullock J. A. and Coppola D. P., *Introduction to Emergency Management*, Fourth Edition (Massachusetts: Butterworth-Heinemann, 2011).

34. Ibid.

35. See note 32 above.

36. See note 6 above.

37. Tyska L. A. and Fennelly L. J., *Physical Security: 150 Things You should Know* (Massachusetts: Butterworth-Heinemann, 2000).

38. Ibid.

39. See note 13 above.

40. Egan M., *The Executive Guide to Information Security: Threats, Challenges, and Solutions* (Indianapolis: Addison-Wesley, 2005).

41. Ibid.
42. See note 21 above.
43. Patterson T., *Mapping Security* (New Jersey: Addison-Wesley, 2005).
44. Ibid.
45. See note 21 above.
46. Andress J., *The Basics of Information Security* (Waltham: Elsevier, 2011).
47. Ibid.
48. Ibid.
49. Ibid, p. 5.
50. Ibid.
51. Ibid.
52. Ibid.
53. Ibid.
54. Ibid.
55. Ibid.
56. Ibid.
57. Ibid.

Evaluating Risk

4

Before you can even think about protecting your facility you need to thoroughly understand the unique risks to it. This involves conducting a risk assessment and physical security survey. This will help you identify weaknesses in your current security system and devise ways to strengthen it.

Risk

Risk has many definitions. Risk, according to Webster's dictionary as a noun is defined as "exposure to possible loss or injury" or "someone or something that creates or suggests a hazard."[1] As a verb, it means "to expose to danger."[2]

Risk is "the potential for damage or loss of an asset."[3] It is the "uncertainty of financial loss, the variations between actual and expected results, or the probability that a loss has occurred or will occur."[4] Risk can be quantitatively defined as the "measure of the potential damage or loss of an asset based on the probability of an undesirable occurrence."[5] Risk is also synonymous with adverse outcomes that organizations strive to avoid.[6]

Risk is commonly divided into three categories.

1. Personal
2. Property
3. Liability

Risks can also be classified as involuntary or voluntary. Involuntary risk is accepted because there is no reasonable alternative to it or there are more benefits to assuming the risk.[7] Driving to work is an example of involuntary risk. Voluntary risk, such as extreme sports, is a risk an individual willingly takes on.[8] Although voluntary risks are willingly undertaken, there are still ways to reduce risk.

Risk Appetite

Risk appetite refers to how willing an organization is to accept risk and how they handle risks to the institution.

There are several ways to handle risk.

1. Deny
2. Ignore
3. Remove or avoid
4. Reduce

5. Spread
6. Transfer
7. Accept

Deny and ignore are not valid options. Crime exists, and pretending it does not places your institution at greater risk. Instead, you want to remove or reduce risk.

Spreading risk involves housing assets in different locations so an adversary attacking one location cannot take every asset. This is most common with manufacturers who may have multiple factories that each makes a single component or more than one factory that make a component so production may be slowed but not halted if the building is attacked. Religious institutions do not really have the option of spreading risk to multiple locations. However, there are ways they can diffuse risk among multiple areas. When I taught preschool over 10 years ago, we called it the "hand grenade theory" and applied it to teacher location on the playground. Essentially, what it meant was teachers needed to be spread out across the playground and not clustered in one area where a single grenade could wipe them all out. It was the most effective way to watch children across a large area and ensure that if something were to happen, a teacher would be close enough to help. The same principle can be applied to your facility.

Transferring risk typically involves using insurance—such as fire, flood, or health—to cover the replacement costs incurred as a result of loss.[9] However, having insurance does not remove responsibility from the religious institution for reducing risk. In addition, insurance does not prevent incidents from happening and cannot restore a facility's reputation. The best ways to handle risk are to remove or reduce it.

Risk reduction has four major criteria for effectiveness.[10]

1. Measures should be spread around so the benefits are shared as widely as possible.
2. Risks are reduced in relation to people's ability to bear them.
3. Compensation is required to address imbalances among the risks.
4. Measures can only be used where there is support among the people who bear the risks by giving their consent.

Removal or avoidance is accomplished by eliminating the source of risk. Reduction is "achieved by taking some actions to lower risk to the enterprise to reduce the severity of the loss," and it is also known as mitigation.[11] Lowering risk by implementing some security measures should be the goal of your security programs.

Ways to Handle Risk

1. Deny
2. Ignore
3. Remove or avoid
4. Reduce
5. Spread
6. Transfer
7. Accept

On some level, there is risk associated with any activity. The recognition that there will always be some residual risk is known as risk acceptance.[12] It is not being defeatist, but it requires actively determining a level of risk that is acceptable to the enterprise.[13] Managing these risks is important to the safety and security of your facility and the people who use it.

Factors that Enhance Chances of Risk Occurring

There are three factors that affect the chances of risk occurring: predictability, probability, and convenience.[14]

1. Predictability
   a. Percentage of chance that one can predict that upcoming events are likely to cause great security risk to persons or organizations.
   b. The greater the risk, the less likely you can predict events leading to that risk.
2. Probability
   a. Reflects what is historically known and is directly related to risk.
   b. Takes into consideration the likelihood of an incident occurring based on the number of actual occurrences of incidents in the past.
   c. Considered more of a true indicator than predictability because it is based on actual history and empirical evidence.
3. Convenience
   a. Being able to provide the necessary measures and strategies while not inconveniencing the persons or the organization to an unacceptable degree.
   b. The more convenient it is, the less secure the person(s) or organization is.

Risk Management

Risk is determined by a combination of elements including the probability of a hazard occurring, the level of exposure of people and property, and the effects—both direct and indirect—of exposure.[15] Therefore, risk estimation "involves developing simple scenarios for hazards and vulnerabilities to them, and gauging the level of exposure of vulnerable items."[16]

Risk management is a methodology for protecting assets by identifying vulnerabilities or weaknesses and strengthening them to reduce the risk to an organization at an acceptable cost. Elements that help a facility reduce risk include creating a security plan, installing physical and/or electronic security countermeasures, increasing security awareness, and establishing security policies and procedures.

Risk management has several goals as outlined by Roper (1999):[17]

1. Ensure that various security recommendations are based on an integrated assessment of loss impacts, threats, vulnerabilities, and resource constraints.
2. Give an understanding of basic concepts involved and their principles.
3. Develop and increase personal awareness in terms of the potential loss impact, threat, and vulnerabilities to your organizational assets.
4. Develop and increase an organizational awareness of security in terms of potential loss impacts, threats, and vulnerabilities.
5. Ensure that security recommendations to senior management decision-makers are based on an integrated assessment of loss impacts, threats, vulnerabilities, and customer resource constraints.

A thorough risk assessment justifies the implementation of security measures and their associated costs. Risk management has many advantages.[18]

1. Provides accountability and consistency.
2. Adaptable for integration with existing tools.
3. Flexible enough to be used within a variety of organizations, facilities, and customers.
4. Identifies critical assets in need of protection.
5. Assesses various types of threats to assets.
6. Determines site-specific vulnerabilities related to a particular type of threat.
7. Determines the consequences or ramifications of undesirable events upon continuing operations.
8. Estimates relative risk levels associated with specific undesirable events.
9. Identifies specific risk mitigation activities and countermeasures to reduce the likelihood of an undesirable event.
10. Analyzes costs and benefits of various risk mitigation strategies.
11. Develops a communication strategy to present risk analysis results, countermeasure options, and recommendations to management and clients/customers.

Within security there are five disciplines that must be considered in any risk management program.[19]

1. Physical
2. Personnel
3. Information
4. Communications
5. Technical, i.e., computer, technical countermeasures, etc.

Risk management is a continuous process that must be completed at regular intervals, including when new threats emerge, and when new technologies or counter-measures are implemented.

Risk Analysis

Risk analysis involves the study of risk conditions and its probable impacts of future incidents.[20] Risk analysis looks at risk estimation and compares different risks and their causes.[21] It is concerned with hazard, vulnerability, and degree of exposure to danger.[22] The study of risk "drives mitigation initiatives to prioritize actions to reduce either the probability that an event will occur or lessen the consequences should it happen."[23]

Risk Assessment

Risk assessment is a process or methodology used to calculate risk or the likelihood that a particular event will occur.[24] Risk has three parts that must be taken into account for a valid evaluation to be made. The first is the probability and frequency of a hazard occurring. The second is the level of exposure of people and property to the hazard. And, finally, the direct and indirect costs or effects of this exposure must be calculated.[25]

For any methodology to be successful, there are certain essential elements or steps that must be undertaken.[26] First, the hazard must be identified and characterized. Whether or not it triggers other hazards must also be evaluated. Second, the frequency and severity of each hazard must be determined. Included in this is the evaluation of which factors, if any, can actually influence the severity of the hazard. Third, the risk must be estimated and its potential effects on the human environment analyzed.

The fourth step is to determine potential economic/direct and societal effects and the indirect effects on costs. Costs include rental and/or relocation, loss of inventory, income loss, repair or replacement, and related loss of function costs.[27] Social costs must be considered as well. These include casualties, injuries, and displacement. Indirect economic effects, although more difficult to obtain data on and calculate, are just as important. They can include increase in unemployment, business interruption, loss of production, reduction in demand and spending, and tax base losses.[28] In a religious institution, this may include decrease in attendance and reduction in charitable donations and contributions.

Two other steps should also be included in a risk assessment methodology. One is determining the acceptable level of risk.[29] After risk is calculated by steps one through four, it can be determined how much risk will be tolerated. There is some risk in everything, but there can be severe political and societal consequences of taking or not taking certain actions to address risks.[30] Last, risk-reduction opportunities must be identified. This involves making decisions, devising strategies, and implementing plans to safeguard persons and property.

Steps in Risk Assessment

1. Describe facility and its users
2. Perform security survey
3. Identify assets and consequences of loss
4. Identify vulnerabilities or weaknesses
5. Identify threats and rank in order of likelihood and criticality
6. Identify countermeasures
7. Perform cost-benefit analysis

Facility Characterization

The first step in evaluating risk is to fully understand and describe your facility. This will help with additional steps of identifying assets, vulnerabilities, and threats. A thorough description of the facility involves the following general areas as outlined by Garcia:[31]

1. Physical conditions
2. Environmental elements
3. Facility operations
4. Policies and procedures

5. Regulatory and legal requirements
6. Safety considerations
7. Legal issues
8. Organizational goals and objectives
We are adding three more to the list as they are of particular importance to securing religious institutions.
9. Facility demographics
10. Services provided
11. Community demographics

As the facility is described in more detail, additional areas of interest may emerge that will lead to further areas of investigation.

Interviewing staff, and even a sample of attendees, will provide valuable information on the facility and its operation as well as perceived threats and vulnerabilities. This process can often uncover facility operations, policies, or procedures that are unknown to some subsets of employees.[32]

Physical Conditions

The physical conditions describe the structure of the facility and existing physical security measures. These features include the following[33]:

1. Site boundaries
2. Number and locations of buildings
3. Off-site locations
4. Room types and their location within each building
5. Access points (entrances)
6. Existing physical protection features
7. Infrastructure details
  a. Heating, ventilation, and air conditioning system (HVAC)
  b. Communication paths and types
  c. Construction materials of walls and ceilings
  d. Power distribution system
  e. Locations of any hazardous materials including cleaning products
  f. Exterior areas

A thorough review of the existing physical conditions will also help in identifying vulnerabilities in your facility's security. The spectrum of risks is as follows in order from highest risk to lowest.

1. Without protection: No security measures at all are in place, such as leaving doors unlocked.[34]
2. Minimum: Some measures such as locked doors and fences are present, but they are easily breached by an adversary.[35]
3. Low-level: Security measures require modest adversary effort to breach, such as alarm systems and reinforced windows and doors.[36]
4. Medium: System impedes, detects, and assesses most unauthorized external and some internal activity, such as monitored alarm systems and unarmed security officers.[37]

5. High-level: This includes features of lower levels as well as CCTV, access controls, advanced sensors, and highly trained and supported security officers.[38]
6. Exceptional: This impedes, detects, assesses, and neutralizes most unauthorized external and internal activity using tamper-resistant, complex systems and highly trained and vetted personnel.[39]
7. Failsafe: This includes a conceptual level of security that is cost-prohibitive and impractical in most situations due to its deliberately restrictive and time-consuming nature.[40]

Environmental Elements

An assessment of the environmental elements in your facility will also aid in determining vulnerabilities. Some of these elements include the following[41]:

1. Topography
2. Vegetation
3. Wildlife
4. Background noise sources
5. Climate
6. Weather
7. Soil
8. Pavement

Understanding these elements will be important when choosing countermeasures as they can decrease the effectiveness of certain elements of a physical protection system. For example, wildlife may set off intrusion detection alarms, vegetation can obscure camera views, and background noise sources can cause false alarms in electronic security systems.

Facility Operations

Facility operations concern what activities are conducted at your facility, who participates in those activities, and when those activities occur. Some of these include the following[42]:

1. Access control methods, systems, and procedures
2. Hours of operation
3. Who uses the facility

An understanding of facility operations is an important part of identifying vulnerabilities.

Policies and Procedures

Policies and procedures are how activities are conducted at your facility. These can include the following:

1. Hiring
2. Emergency response
3. Volunteer management
4. Community outreach
5. Money handling

6. Food handling and distribution
7. Space reservation and/or rental

These may be formal or informal as well as written or unwritten. However, to protect you from liability as well as to improve your security, they should be both formal and written.

Regulatory and Legal Requirements

You should be familiar with regulatory requirements, building codes, industry standards, and legal requirements that pertain to your facility. This may include those that apply to only a small part such as the kitchen or day care. Review your insurance policies as well for exemptions, prohibitions, and exceptions.

Safety Considerations

Safety is closely aligned with security. You need to look at these issues carefully to ensure that you do not sacrifice one for the other. For example, you should not block fire exit doors or chain them closed.

Legal Issues

Chapter 13 discusses liability issues that could affect your organization.

Organizational Goals and Objectives

Security should never interfere with the mission of your organization. However, avoiding all security measures is unacceptable.

Facility Demographics

What are the characteristics of those who use your facility? What age groups do you service? What is their educational level and socioeconomic status? The answers to these questions can influence the types of threats your facility can experience.

Services Provided

1. Religious
2. Counseling
3. Food collection and distribution
4. Soup kitchens
5. Fund-raising
6. Bill-paying

Community Demographics

The location of your facility is also important to understanding threats and vulnerabilities. You should answer the following questions:

1. Is your facility located in a commercial or residential neighborhood?
2. Does your property adjoin the property of other businesses or residences?

3. Do you share common areas with other residences or businesses such as sidewalks or parking lots?
4. Do the religious leaders live on site or nearby?
5. Does anyone live on the premises or nearby such as caretakers, facility maintenance workers, landscapers, etc?

Security Survey

Conducting a security survey provides understanding of the current state of the security program. It focuses on five primary areas: the perimeter, entrances, the interior, security planning, and interior design.

For each category, you should look at the following categories: minimum standards, observations, concerns, and recommendations. Minimum standards can be building codes, state or federal regulations, or any other criteria set by a standard-setting organization. Observations are a description of the current security measures or lack thereof. Concerns are the perceived weaknesses and vulnerabilities. Recommendations are the countermeasures, whether operational, physical, or electronic, suggested for implementation.

Your facility may have some or all of these elements. It may also have elements not described in this section. Elements of the perimeter that should be evaluated include boundaries, parking areas, physical barriers, CCTV, and alarm systems, outside lighting, landscaping, and proximity to other buildings. Entrances include access control, intrusion detection, personnel or baggage screening, receiving and shipping, lobby, and windows.

The interior focuses on employee and visitor identification, stairwells, elevators, utilities, interior lighting, HVAC system, fire alarm system and sprinklers, roof access, and backup generators. Interior design is another element for evaluation. It includes doors, hallways, room layouts, and other elements of interior design.

Another important area of evaluation is security planning. This includes emergency preparedness plans, continuity-of-operations, new-hire and volunteer screening, and any other policies and procedures that could impact security either positively or negatively.

A thorough evaluation of the current security posture of your facility will influence countermeasure selection. It will also show if you need to renovate existing systems, upgrade them, or install brand new ones.

Identifying Assets

Identifying assets, also called target identification, is the basis for designing a security program. It is an evaluation of what to protect, i.e., those elements whose loss will have negative consequences for the facility or those elements that have a positive value to their owner.

Assets can be divided into six general categories: people, activities, information, buildings, financial instruments, and property. These assets can be tangible or intangible. Tangible assets include people, property, and the facility itself. Intangible assets include information, activities, and reputations.

Once identified, the value of each asset must be calculated. First, its value is assessed based upon its value to the owner.[43] Then, value is reassessed based on its worth to an adversary. Although it may also have a level of value to both an adversary and its owner, the nature and magnitude of those values can differ dramatically.[44]

Keep in mind, however, that there are other ways to calculate the worth of an asset other than in financial terms. The value of an asset could also be calculated in terms of human life or quality of life, the effect on organizational interests, the impact on organizational survival, the consequences to political or national interests, or the influence on goodwill and reputation.[45] Although values can be calculated by methods other than pure dollar amounts, all calculations will affect profit in the long run. However, if a given asset has no real value to an adversary or its owner, it is probably not necessary to protect it.

Figure 4.1 shows typical assets of religious institutions. Use this chart as a guide, but add or subtract items as necessary.

The location of assets is also important. Identify areas that house items of value or a sensitive nature.[46] These areas will require additional protective measures.

1. **People**: People are the single most important asset your facility has. If they do not feel safe, they will go elsewhere.
2. **Property**: This includes the facility itself, church property such as computers, and the personal property of attendees such as wallets, GPS systems, and cell phones.
3. **Information**: Examples are home addresses and amount of money collected.

Assets		Value
People	Staff Volunteers Attendees Visitors Other Users	$ inestimable
Activities	Childcare Services Community Outreach Counseling School	$ inestimable
Information	Schedules and hours of operation Attendee names, addresses, email, and phone numbers Financial information	$ inestimable
Buildings	Main building Off site locations Other buildings such as storage units, tool sheds, etc.	Monetary Value
Property	Computers Audiovisual Equipment Instruments Appliances Vehicles Art Other Items	Monetary Value
Intangible Capital	Reputation Relationships Goodwill Faith	$ inestimable

Figure 4.1 Typical assets of a religious institution.

Identifying Threats and Adversaries

Threat identification is the cornerstone of any risk assessment. The countermeasures chosen for a facility are dependent upon the type of threat they must protect against.

A threat is "any indication, circumstance, or event with the potential to cause the loss of or damage to an asset" or the "intention and capability of an adversary to undertake actions that would be detrimental to the interests of the asset owner."[47]

Threats are categorized as either natural or man-made. Natural threats refer to natural disasters that cause damage.[48] Man-made threats are not caused by nature and are, thus, less consistent and predictable than natural threats.[49] Security is primarily concerned with man-made threats, whereas natural disasters impact the safety of the organization.

Security measures are based on certain assumptions about the capabilities, intentions, methods, and other characteristics of perceived adversaries. To ensure the accuracy and efficiency of security measures, it is necessary to identify the most likely threats to the religious institution.

A threat definition is a detailed description of the threat posed by an adversary and should include information concerning their potential actions; motivations; tactics such as force, stealth, or deceit; potential goals based upon targets; and physical capabilities such as tools, experience, number, and weapons.[50]

Threats can come from three areas: insiders, outsiders, and insiders colluding with outsiders. Most facilities are more aware of, and therefore prepared for, outsider threats. These include criminals, hate groups, and others who have no real ties to the facility.

Insider threats come from those who have a legitimate reason to be in your facility such as leaders, staff, and attendees. They use that connection to commit criminal activity. These threats can include financial managers who embezzle money, youth ministers who molest children, and those who skim funds from donations. Research indicates that the majority of violent acts are carried out by those who have a current or former connection.[51] Insiders are distinguished from other adversaries by knowledge of the system; they have authorized access to the assets, physical protection system (PPS), or the facility without raising suspicion; and they have the time to choose the opportunity to commit an act.[52] The most probable threat is a single insider as they "are responsible for the majority of security breaches in both physical and computer security systems."[53]

Insiders colluding with outsiders are the third type of threat. This includes staff that let others know the location of items that can be sold for money or ways to defeat the security system. An insider can help an outsider adversary in many ways. First of all, they are privy to information about the working of the physical protection system and may even know how to turn off alarm systems or where the hidden cameras are located. They have legitimate access to information that can be given to an outsider to be used in a criminal act. White-collar crimes such as identity theft, bank fraud, armored car robberies, embezzlement, and insider trading can all be accomplished by insiders working with outsiders or an insider by his or her self.[54]

Threats will depend upon the mission and location of the facility and information should be gathered on the local, regional, national, and international levels.[55] This should include a "review and characterization of the local and national population" as any discontented or disgruntled faction of the population can be a potential adversary.[56]

Threat identification is a time-consuming process and can be difficult to attain. "Understanding threats requires an understanding of the adversaries' perspective, in terms of their intentions and motives, as well as their capabilities to compromise the assets."[57] This can be extremely difficult to determine as it "requires making assumptions and speculations based on bits and pieces of information that may not be complete."[58] In addition, a single facility often faces multiple threats, although they may differ with regard to motivation, capability, tactics, probability, vulnerability, and severity of impact.

The goals, motivations, and other important factors may differ depending on the type of adversary, but they can be categorized into three basic groups: ideological, economic, and personal—regardless if the adversaries are insiders or outsiders.[59] Ideological threats include groups such as extremists, fanatics, or political terrorists whose motives are linked to a political or philosophical system. Economic threats come from criminals motivated for financial gain such as theft, embezzlement, or robbery. Personal motivations pertain to specific situations of specific individuals, such as hostile employees with a grievance, psychotic individuals, hackers, and drug/alcohol abuse.

Identifying Undesirable Events

Once threats or potential adversaries have been identified, the next step is to identify undesirable events, in other words, what harm each adversary can bring to each asset. Undesirable events include robbery, vandalism, natural disaster, fraud, loss of reputation, or an active shooter situation.

Events are rated based on likelihood and impact. Those two factors are multiplied to create the relative weight of the event. Once events are all given relative weights, they can then be ranked according to criticality.

1 = Very Low
2 = Low
3 = Medium
4 = High
5 = Very High

Impact is rated as follows:

1 = Negligible
2 = Some
3 = Moderate
4 = Significant
5 = Severe

Identifying Consequences or Impact of Undesirable Events

Now you know what you want to protect, who your potential adversaries are, and how they can harm your assets. The next step is to identify the consequences of loss or damage to these assets. You should evaluate how each undesirable event could impact each asset.

Impact includes both direct and indirect costs.[60] Costs do not necessarily imply financial consequences and may be qualitative instead of quantitative. Direct costs are casualties, injuries, and loss of property. Indirect costs may be more difficult to calculate and obtain. These costs may include loss of reputation and psychological trauma to the victims. Indirect costs are often not immediately apparent and can manifest in the weeks or months following an incident.

The duration of impact can also affect the costs. It is dependent upon several factors: type of hazard, the severity of its effects, and the size of the area affected.[61] Typically, the longer the duration, the higher the impact or costs will be.

Loss estimation can be calculated by looking at the most likely loss scenarios for your facility. It is common to base loss estimates on previous events to provide a baseline. However, it is important to recognize that "although the physical variables remain the same, the losses will vary in relation to changes in vulnerability that have occurred in the area since the last damaging event."[62]

Loss can be calculated in three ways: casualties, structural damages, and economic or productivity losses. Economic losses are somewhat dependent upon the estimates of casualties and structural damages as loss of workers or building space negatively impacts productivity. Casualties are the most difficult to estimate as they are dependent upon levels of concentration of humans in a particular area as well as the efficiency of evacuation procedures.[63] In addition, higher levels of damage tend to cause more significant numbers of injuries and increase the severity of those injuries.[64]

Financial or economic losses can be calculated as both short-term and long-term losses. Short-term losses are the immediate consequences of the event. Long-term consequences must also be factored into financial losses through lost transactions, lost income, and costs of reconstruction and aid.[65] Do not underestimate costs due to the nonprofit nature of your institution. You still have employees, materials, equipment, property, goods, and services that engender costs.

Identifying Vulnerabilities

Vulnerability is "any weakness that can be exploited by an adversary to gain access to an asset."[66] It may result from equipment properties, building characteristics, operational and personnel practices, personnel behavior, and locations of people, equipment, and buildings.[67]

Building characteristics may include having an all-glass atrium or a side entrance without a lock. Equipment properties are flaws in the equipment itself, such as metal detectors that are useless in detecting plastic explosives. Personnel behavior can be closely tied to operational practices, such as the individual who monitors the security cameras also having to check employee and visitor identification. Every second they are looking at people leaves the cameras unattended. It would be easy for someone to distract them while an accomplice performs an unlawful act that would have been caught on the camera monitors. Locations of equipment can be an issue as well, particularly if the fire alarm control room is located near a door that has no guard stationed there or no lock.

Vulnerability can also be calculated from the probability that an attack on a specific component will be successful, and it is the "measure of the strength of a component in the face of a threat."[68] Vulnerability analysis also has to take into account the interplay among components as they can result in secondary threats or cascading failures.[69]

Religious institutions have unique vulnerabilities that make them attractive targets to certain criminals. Common vulnerabilities include hours of operation, childcare, demographics, use of volunteers, and community outreach services such as counseling services, food banks, financial assistance, and helping disadvantaged groups.

Members and staff do not have a security mind-set and lack a security consciousness. They do not believe anyone would violate the sanctity of a house of worship. As a result, they may inadvertently contribute to vulnerability.

Hours of operation can be a weakness as many religious institutions operate at varied hours but are often open yet vacant.[70] Activity schedules are predictable and advertised, alerting potential violators to optimal times for criminal activity.[71]

Users of the facility include vulnerable groups such as children, youth, and elderly, which can further complicate security matters. A reliance on volunteers and staffing from members can be a significant risk as well. Playgrounds, schools, and day care centers present additional risks and challenges to the overall security of a facility. In addition, special events such as weddings, funerals, and baptisms often bring in outsiders who are unknown to members, making it easy for a perpetrator to slip in unnoticed.

What areas of the facility are most vulnerable?

- Parking lots
- Restrooms
- Childcare facilities
- Playground
- Offsite locations
- Vehicles
- Areas where money is handled
- Stairwells

Choosing Countermeasures

Once you know what needs to be protected and who it needs to be protected from, you can choose countermeasures. Your security survey will have identified the weaknesses and vulnerabilities in your current security program. It is best to start with what you have and add procedures, personnel, and equipment as necessary.

Chapter 5 explains various physical and electronic security countermeasures in more detail. However, a few examples are included here. To counter loss of property, control of and accounting for assets must be established.[72] This can be established through use of procedures, tracking, audits, and inventories.[73]

Pre-employment screening is one of the best ways to gauge honesty and trustworthiness, but it is not foolproof.[74] Access control through the use of badges or strict key control can prevent employees from gaining access to areas in which they have no business.[75] Good supervision of employees by management as well as training managers to detect suspicious employee behavior are additional ways to reduce insider threats.[76]

"As redundant layers of effective security countermeasures are applied, the likelihood of successful exploitation drops, since the vulnerabilities, and consequently the risk, are reduced or eliminated."[77] Countermeasures in their relation to vulnerability can be ranked in order of most vulnerable to least.

1. Critical: "no effective countermeasures currently in place and it would be extremely easy for adversaries to exploit weaknesses."[78]
2. High: "although there are some countermeasures in place, there are still multiple weaknesses through which adversaries would be capable of exploiting an asset."[79]
3. Medium: "while there are effective countermeasures in place, one weakness does exist which adversaries would have considerable difficulty exploiting the asset."[80]
4. Low: "multiple layers of effective countermeasures exist, and adversaries would have considerable difficulty exploiting the asset."[81]

Cost-Benefit Analysis

Recommended countermeasures have associated costs that can be measured in terms of dollars, inconvenience, time, or personnel. Cost-benefit analysis is a powerful tool for defining risk-reduction strategies as well as convincing leaders to fund them.[82] Cost-benefit analysis can reveal that natural disasters involve disproportionately large losses.[83]

Another important aspect of this analysis is that it can identify the marginal point of diminishing returns, which is the point at which additional money will not actually reduce risk.[84] This helps set a balanced budget allowing for allocation of just the right amount of funding needed to be successful.

A good risk analysis can show how funds should be allocated to reduce risk. There are five basic strategies that can be applied to protecting facilities from damages.[85] Network-wide investment gives a damage estimate for every component in a system.[86] Ranked allocation funds the highest ranking or most vulnerable components first. Apportioned allocation offers funds for as many components as possible but in differing amounts if necessary.[87] Optimal allocation seeks to minimize vulnerability or risk by allocating funds where they will do the most good.[88] Manual allocation is completed by a policy maker and may not necessarily be the most optimal solution.[89]

There are a few things to keep in mind when performing a cost-benefit analysis. Many of the vulnerabilities of a facility are due to policies and procedures, which can be improved at a negligible cost. Improvements can often be made to existing elements of the physical protection system that will further strengthen the security of the facility. These costs would be significantly less than installing brand new systems.

Putting It All Together

Now that your analysis has been completed, you will need to present it to leaders who have the authority to accept or deny requests for security. A formal risk analysis report summarizes the findings of the risk assessment and presents recommendations for improving security.

Formal Risk Analysis Report

1. Introduction
   a. Scope
   b. Summary
   c. Purpose
2. Executive summary
3. Facility characterization
4. Threats/potential adversaries
5. Vulnerabilities/weaknesses
6. Specify loss risk events/vulnerabilities
7. Establish the probability of loss risk and frequency of events
8. Determine the impact of the event
9. Develop options to mitigate risks
10. Study the feasibility of implementation of options
11. Perform a cost/benefit analysis

Final Thoughts

A risk assessment is a comprehensive evaluation of your facility that enables you to identify your risks, rank them in order of criticality, and identify ways to mitigate them. One of the most important things to realize—as I'm sure we all do—is that funding is limited. As a result, assets must be prioritized as you may only be able to allocate funds to the most critical and vulnerable asset(s). Risk assessment can help a facility identify and prioritize these assets.

A proper risk assessment is crucial to the security of your facility and the foundation for your security efforts. It can be a daunting task, but if you follow the steps, you can understand the strengths of your facility and the risks to it. Then, you can design and implement an effective security program.

End Notes

1. Merriam-Webster, *Webster's All-In-One Dictionary and Thesaurus*, Second Edition (Springfield: Federal Street Press, 2013).
2. Ibid.
3. Roper C. A., *Risk Management for Security Professionals* (Boston: Butterworth-Heinemann, 1999), 13.
4. Sennewald C. A., *Effective Security Management*, Fourth Edition (Boston: Butterworth-Heinemann, 2003), 193.
5. Garcia M. L., *The Design and Evaluation of Physical Protection Systems*, Second Edition (Boston: Butterworth-Heinemann, 2008), 300.
6. McGlown K. J., *Terrorism and Disaster Management: Preparing Healthcare Leaders for the New Reality* (Chicago: Health Administration Press, 2004).

7. Alexander D., *Principles of Emergency Planning and Management* (New York: Oxford University Press, 2002).

8. Ibid.

9. Garcia M. L., *The Design and Evaluation of Physical Protection Systems*, Second Edition (Boston: Butterworth-Heinemann, 2008).

10. See note 7 above.

11. See note 9 above, p. 272.

12. See note 9 above.

13. See note 9 above.

14. Fennelly Lawrence J., *Effective Physical Security*, Third Edition (Boston: Butterworth-Heinemann, 2004).

15. Haddow G. D., Bullock J. A. and Coppola D. P., *Introduction to Emergency Management*, Fourth Edition (Boston: Butterworth-Heinemann, 2011).

16. See note 7 above, p. 58.

17. Roper C. A., *Risk Management for Security Professionals* (Boston: Butterworth-Heinemann, 1999).

18. Ibid.

19. Ibid.

20. See note 7 above.

21. See note 7 above.

22. See note 7 above.

23. See note 6 above, p. 41.

24. See note 15 above.

25. See note 15 above.

26. See note 15 above.

27. See note 15 above.

28. See note 15 above.

29. See note 15 above.

30. See note 15 above.

31. See note 9 above.

32. See note 9 above.

33. See note 9 above.

34. McCrie R. D., *Security Operations Management*, Second Edition (Boston: Butterworth-Heinemann, 2007).

35. Ibid.

36. Ibid.

37. Ibid.

38. Ibid.

39. Ibid.

40. Ibid.

41. See note 9 above.

42. See note 9 above.

43. See note 17 above.

44. See note 17 above.

45. See note 17 above.

46. Tyska L. A. and Fennelly L. J., *Physical Security: 150 Things You should Know* (Massachusetts: Butterworth-Heinemann, 2000).

47. See note 3 above.

48. Kovacich G. L., *The Manager's Handbook for Corporate Security* (Boston: Butterworth-Heinemann, 2003).
49. Ibid.
50. See note 9 above.
51. Burk T., Weiss J. and Davis M., "Church Protectors," *The Journal of Counter Terrorism and Homeland Security International* 20, no. 2 (2014): 36–39.
52. See note 9 above.
53. See note 9 above, p. 27.
54. See note 34 above.
55. See note 9 above.
56. See note 9 above, p. 30.
57. See note 17 above, p. 44.
58. Ibid.
59. See note 9 above.
60. See note 15 above.
61. See note 7 above.
62. See note 7 above, p. 64.
63. See note 7 above.
64. See note 7 above.
65. See note 7 above.
66. See note 17 above, p. 14.
67. See note 17 above.
68. Lewis T. G., *Critical Infrastructure Protection in Homeland Security: Defending a Networked Nation* (New Jersey: John Wiley & Sons, Inc., 2006), 108.
69. Lewis T. G., *Critical Infrastructure Protection in Homeland Security: Defending a Networked Nation* (New Jersey: John Wiley & Sons, Inc, 2006).
70. Quarles C. L. and Ratliff P. L., *Crime Prevention for Houses of Worship* (Alexandria: American Society for Industrial Security, 2001).
71. American Crime Prevention Institute, *Church Crime Prevention*, 2008. Retrieved from http://www.santarosa.fl.gov/coad/documents/ChurchCrimePreventionVSept2008.pdf.
72. See note 9 above.
73. See note 9 above.
74. Patterson D. G., *Implementing Physical Protection Systems: A Practical Guide* (Alexandria: ASIS International, 2004).
75. See note 14 above.
76. See note 74 above.
77. See note 17 above, 69.
78. See note 17 above, p. 70.
79. Ibid.
80. Ibid.
81. Ibid.
82. See note 7 above.
83. See note 7 above.
84. See note 7 above.
85. See note 69 above.
86. See note 69 above.
87. See note 69 above.
88. See note 69 above.
89. See note 69 above.

Choosing Physical and Electronic Security Countermeasures

Once the risk assessment is completed, the next step is to choose security countermeasures, both physical and electronic. Countermeasures refer to any "action taken or a physical entity used to reduce or eliminate one or more vulnerabilities."[1] Countermeasures seek to reduce costs associated with loss. These costs are not limited to monetary ones, but may include reduced operational efficiency, adverse publicity, unfavorable working conditions, and political consequences.[2] Countermeasures include physical protection systems and response forces as well as operational procedures.[3] There are a variety of countermeasures available, but the measures you choose are dependent upon the type of threat, the asset to be protected, and the overall vulnerability of the asset.

A **physical protection system** (PPS) is composed of people, procedures/processes, and equipment/technology that are integrated to provide protection against malevolent human acts.[4] To create an effective system, the objectives must be weighed against available resources. Without a careful assessment, the system may waste valuable resources on unnecessary protection or fail to provide adequate protection where needed.[5]

Security System Functions

A good security system has several functions—detection, delay, and response—that must accomplish the goal of protecting assets from a malevolent adversary.[6] These functions are tied together in the following manner. For a system to be effective, "there must be awareness that there is an attack (detection) and slowing of adversary progress to the targets (delay), thus allowing the response force enough time to interrupt or stop the adversary."[7] These functions are applied as an integrated combination of people, procedures, and equipment to meet the protection objectives and the needs of the facility.

Detection, or the discovery of an adversary action, includes sensing of covert or overt actions.[8] Effectiveness of the detection function is measured as "the probability of sensing adversary action and the time required for reporting and assessing the alarm."[9] Access control, defined as "allowing entry to authorized personnel and detecting the attempted entry of unauthorized personnel and material," is included in the detection function.[10]

Delay, which is the slowing down of adversarial progress, can be accomplished through barriers, fences, locks, personnel, and other methods.[11] In order to be effective, delay must occur after detection.[12] Delay that occurs prior to detection does not offer any value to the responding team, but it does function as a deterrent. The measure of its effectiveness is "the time required by the adversary (after detection) to bypass each element."[13]

Response is the set of actions taken by responding forces to prevent adversary progress and is accomplished primarily through interruption. It includes communication of accurate information as well as deployment of the responding force.[14] Response effectiveness is measured as "the time between receipt of a communication of adversary action and the interruption of the adversary action."[15]

Deployment is part of the response function. It is defined as "the actions of the response force from the time communication is received until the force is in position to interrupt the adversary."[16] Effectiveness is measured as "the probability of deployment to the adversary location and the time required to deploy the response force."[17]

The objectives of a system are based on the function of the security measures. In addition to detect, delay, and response, there are the following.

1. **Prevent**: concerns ways to keep an event from ever happening
2. **Deter**: components that make the facility look like an unattractive target so they will go elsewhere
3. **Deny**: components that block an adversary from reaching their goal
4. **Detain**: components that not only slow an adversary's progress but hold them in place until a response force can intercept them
5. **Assess**: components that allow a response force to determine the nature of an alarm in order to make a decision on how to respond
6. **Investigate**: components that allow for investigation of incidents after they have occurred such as CCTV
7. **Communicate**: components that allow members of a security team to share vital information about threats
8. **Mitigate**: components that lessen the impact, damage, or loss associated with a particular threat

These functions often overlap, and a single countermeasure may perform multiple functions. For example, a fence may both deter and deny an adversary.

Designing and Implementing a Physical Protection System

When designing a security system, planning is important to assure that it meets your needs. The following format, as outlined by Patterson, can be used whether you are looking for one particular element of a system or are designing an entire system comprised of multiple technologies.[18]

1. Planning
   a. Threat assessment vulnerability analysis
   b. Recommended safeguards
   c. PPS requirements document
   d. Procurement method
   e. Sole source justification
   f. Business objectives
   g. Design criteria
   h. Design requirements

     i. Performance requirements
     j. Capacity requirements
2. Design
     a. Contract information
     b. Bidders' instructions
     c. System specifications
     d. Evaluation criteria
     e. Implementation schedule
     f. Equipment lists
     g. Security devices schedules
     h. Door hardware
     i. CCTV camera schedule
     j. Drawings
3. Estimation
     a. Budgetary estimates
     b. Preliminary design estimates
     c. Final design estimates
     d. Life cycle cost estimates
     e. Schedules and time frames
4. Procurement
     a. Bidders' conference
     b. Technical evaluations
     c. Cost evaluations
     d. Interview results
     e. Due diligence results
     f. Contract
5. Installation and Operation
     a. Factory test plan
     b. Acceptance test plan
     c. Training syllabus
     d. Training manuals
     e. Maintenance procedures
     f. Factory acceptance tests
     g. Site acceptance tests
     h. As-built drawings
     i. Operating procedures
     j. Response procedures
     k. Product data.
     l. Commissioning plan
     m. Acceptance test results
     n. Punch list
     o. Project completion certificate
6. Training
     a. Training manuals
     b. Audiovisuals
     c. Lesson plans
     d. Agendas
     e. Schedules
     f. Training class evaluations

7. Testing and Warranty Issues
   a. Predelivery or factory acceptance test data
   b. Site acceptance test data
   c. Review of operations logs and records
   d. Warranty plan
   e. Warranty reports
   f. Warranty records
   g. Upgrades
8. Maintenance, Evaluation, and Replacement
   a. Maintenance records
   b. Trouble records
   c. Review of operations logs and records
   d. Upgrades
   e. Operating costs and maintenance records
   f. Replacement study

Phases of Design and Implementation

1. Planning
2. Design
3. Estimation
4. Procurement
5. Installation and Operation
6. Training
7. Testing and Warranty Issues
8. Maintenance, Evaluation, and Replacement

Adversary Factors to Consider in PPS Design

An important part of designing a system of countermeasures is to consider certain characteristics of the potential threats—capability, tactics, and potential actions.[19] Adversary capabilities include experience, number, type of weapons, and the tools they use. Tactics include force, stealth, and deceit.[20] Potential actions, as discussed in Chapter 4, are the undesirable events that an adversary could cause.

Types of Countermeasures

There are a variety of elements that can be used to create a security system. An excellent resource on the subject is Mary Lynn Garcia's *The Design and Evaluation of Physical Protection Systems*. That book goes into more detail than we will here.

Exterior Intrusion Sensors

Sensors are an integral part of any physical protection system. Exterior intrusion sensors can be classified using five methods: passive or active; covert or visible; line-of-sight or terrain-following; volumetric or line detection; and by mode of application.[21]

Passive sensors detect energy emitted by the target. Active sensors transmit energy and detect changes created by the presence of the target.[22] Covert are hidden from view, whereas visible are in plain view of adversaries. Sometimes, visible sensors can have a deterrent effect by their mere presence.

Line-of-sight sensors require a clear line of sight, typically a flat ground surface, in order to be effective. However, terrain-following can detect equally well on irregular and flat surfaces.[23]

Volumetric detection senses intrusion into a volume of space, which is typically hard for an intruder to identify. Line detection occurs along a line, such as a fence, and any deviation from that line will sound the alarm.[24] Sensors classified by the mode of application are buried line, fence-associated, or freestanding.

Due to variances in sensitivity and environmental factors, it is important to use several different types of sensors to provide maximum security. This provides balanced protection and reduces overall vulnerability.[25] Different sensors are effective at detecting different types of intrusions and have different vulnerabilities, so using a combination of them will reduce vulnerability more than any single type of sensor.[26] To detect all expected types of intrusion and lower the nuisance alarm rate, a variety of sensors should be used.[27] Different sensors can also adjust for environmental conditions ensuring that at least one system is fully functional at all times. Installing sensors with proper overlap at sector boundaries will prevent blind spots that can be exploited by an adversary.

Nothing prevents you from moving sensors out to the very limits of your property to detect intrusions as early as possible. However, that may not be the best course of action. Sensors that are very far away from the command center will take longer to respond to. If they are false alarms, a great deal of time could be wasted by officers investigating the source of the alarm.

Sensors can also be expensive. It may be cost prohibitive to put motion detectors around 500 acres of land. However, those same sensors can be put around the 40 acres where the important materials and people are housed. Fewer sensors would be needed in a smaller area. It is part of prioritizing security needs and balancing them with costs.

Interior Intrusion Sensors

Interior intrusion sensors use the same classification scheme as exterior sensors. However, their application classes are different. These are boundary-penetration sensors, interior motion sensors, and proximity sensors.[28] As with exterior sensors, interior sensors have different vulnerabilities and detection methods, making it essential to use multiple technologies to protect your critical assets.

Alarm Assessment

The principle that detection is not complete without assessment is "based on the premise that the primary goal of a security system is to protect assets from loss or damage."[29] To meet this objective, there must be the detection of an attack and delay of an adversary that is long enough to allow an appropriate response.[30] It must be determined if the alarm is false or if it signals an attack for an appropriate response to be coordinated.[31] This is where assessment comes in.

Closed-circuit Television Systems (CCTV)

One of the most effective assessment methods is the use of closed-circuit television or CCTV. This type of system allows rapid assessment of alarms at remote locations and avoids unnecessarily sending a response force or patrols to the area.[32]

The essential components of a CCTV or video alarm assessment system include the following:[33]

1. Camera and lens
2. Lighting system
3. Transmission system
4. Video switching equipment
5. Video recorder
6. Video monitor
7. Video controller

Not only does a CCTV system aid in assessment, but it can provide evidence for investigation and prosecution as well if it records information.

The camera resolution needed depends upon the function of the system. Resolution is the ability to see fine details in an image.[34] The higher the resolution, the more detailed the image. The lowest resolution is for detection purposes. Detection is the ability to detect the presence of an object in the area of interest.[35] The next highest resolution is for classification. The camera must provide sufficient detail to determine the class of the object that is present such as an animal, blowing debris, or a person.[36] The highest resolution is for identification, which allows you to identify the object based upon appearance details.[37]

Lighting is also important for camera systems so that images are viewable. The following are characteristics of the interaction between lighting systems and camera systems.[38]

1. Light fixtures should be mounted well above the camera height.
2. The sensitivity of a CCTV camera can be defined as the minimum amount of illumination required to produce a specified signal.
3. Recorded information must meet certain legal standards to be admissible as evidence.
4. Camera selection should be based primarily on the sensitivity required for a full video output signal in the lighting environment in the area to be assessed.
5. The greater the resolution, the greater the spacing between the cameras can be.

Barriers

Barriers are commonly used to delay adversaries. Delays can be placed strategically along an adversary's path, forcing them to choose another way to go.[39] There are many types of barriers available for use in PPS systems. Barriers increase adversary task time by impeding progress along any path that could be chosen, which provides the time necessary for the response force to arrive.[40]

Barriers come in two main types—natural and structural. Natural barriers are topographical features that assist in impeding or denying access to an area such as rivers, cliffs, canyons, or dense growth.[41] Structural barriers are permanent or temporary devices such as fences, walls, grilles, doors, roadblocks, screens, or any other construction that will serve as a deterrent to unauthorized entry.[42] We will focus on structural barriers.

Fences are the most common structural barrier and are typically the outermost protective layer in a PPS system. Fences can vary in type, size, use, and effectiveness. Although fences are not a deterrent to a determined adversary, they do establish a visible legal barrier by marking the extent of a property. Signage warning of trespassing can be mounted on the fence to provide an additional deterrent factor.

Fences can easily be defeated by an adversary. They can be rammed with vehicles, crawled under, climbed over, or cut through.[43] Adding barbed wire can significantly delay penetration time, but it creates an atmosphere that a religious institution likely does not want.

The floor, ceiling, and walls of a room are considered structural barriers as are doors, windows, roofs, and utility ports.[44] Without additional protections, most structural barriers are easily penetrated.

Walls are considered "more resistant to penetration and less desirable as targets for forcible entry than are doors, windows, vents, and other conventional wall openings."[45] Explosives are an effective way to breach walls; however, the amount needed increases substantially with wall thickness.[46] The most effective upgrade for walls is the use of an earthen cover or other overburden such as reinforced concrete to delay access to the wall itself or the use of thick or multiple concrete walls to extend delay time.[47]

Doors are often one of the weakest links in a structure due to their function. As a result, "the principle of balanced design requires that doors and their associated frames, hinges, bolts, and locks be strengthened to afford the same delay as that provided by the floors, walls, and ceilings of the parent structure."[48]

The ultimate value of a barrier is determined by its weakest point, making it essential to ensure that the floor, ceiling, and walls of a room are balanced.[49] A door made of reinforced steel is of little use if it can easily be removed from its hinges. If information or cash are kept in a room, it would necessitate the need for additional protections to the room itself.

Barriers can provide protection against undesirable events if they are properly designed. A chain-link fence may provide protection against an adversary walking into the facility. However, it will not provide protection against an adversary driving a vehicle through it. Bollards protect against vehicle attacks, but do not prevent individuals from walking in with plastic explosives.

Lighting

Lighting is important to camera systems and also in parking lots to ensure that an adversary cannot sneak up on an unsuspecting person. Lighting systems include continuous, standby, moveable, and emergency systems. One facility can use one, all, or a combination of systems.

Continuous (stationary) lights are a set of fixed luminaries that provide continuous illumination during the hours of darkness.[50] They are the most common type.

Standby lights are good for low-priority areas. They are similar to continuous but are need-based, turning on with alarms or by officers.[51]

Movable lights are manually operated—such as search lights—and can supplement continuous or standby lighting.[52]

Emergency lights can duplicate any or all of the above systems, but they are limited to power failures or other emergencies that make other systems inoperative.[53]

Pitfalls to Avoid

It is important to design a system based on the unique characteristics of your particular site. This is known as a site-specific system.[54]There is no one-size-fits-all, as a system designed for one site cannot be transferred to another.

There are other pitfalls to avoid when deciding on security measures. These include one-dimensional security, piecemeal security, reactive security, and packaged security.

One-dimensional security relies on a single deterrent.[55] This is easy to defeat, leaving your facility vulnerable.

Piecemeal security involves adding elements as the need arises without an overall comprehensive plan.[56] While you can add elements as necessary, it is important that they are compatible and integrated into an overall planned system. Some elements may interfere with the effectiveness of other elements.

Reactive security responds to specific loss events.[57] It may be designed for only one specific type of threat. It may also be implemented after an incident has occurred. While security is often reactive, the problem is when it applies only to a specific type of event without taking into account other vulnerabilities and threats.

Packaged security installs standard systems without relation to specific threats.[58] This can involve off-the-shelf packages. The problem with this is that the system does not take into account the specific needs of the facility. It wastes time, money, and other resources without making the facility more secure.

Implementing Physical Security Measures

Once you've decided on the broad categories of physical security measures, classify them according to ease of implementation. Start with what you have and add technology, procedures, and personnel as needed.

1. Measures that can be instituted now with little to no cost
2. Measures that can be implemented within the next 6–12 months with some cost
3. Measures that require a significant outlay of time and/or cost

This classification scheme will help you with the overall security plan. Phasing in security measures will not overwhelm people or budgets.

However, it is important to implement security measures in the proper order. Typically, this is from the outside in. For example, a fence around the property or bollards may be installed before the security cameras or alarm system.

Improving an Existing PPS

If you already have a physical protection system in place, you may simply want to upgrade it after performing your risk assessment. However, there are many things that need to be considered including the following:

1. Costs
    a. Installation
    b. Life cycle
2. Creation of additional vulnerabilities
3. System integration
4. Component compatibility
5. Maintenance impacts
6. Safety issues
7. Policy and procedure changes
8. Cultural impact
9. Increase in manpower
10. Increased training requirements
11. Design life
12. System effectiveness against specified threat
13. Possibly accepting risks associated with having vulnerability in the design

Systems Integration

One of the most important concepts in security is the integration of the various elements of people, technology, and procedures into a cohesive physical protection system. An integrated system is controlled by a single, supervisory computer as opposed to a system of interconnected devices.[59]

A well-integrated system saves the following:[60]

1. Management time
2. Employee training time
3. Response time
4. Physical space
5. Money

Performance Measures for PPS Functions

The performance of a physical protection system can be measured in several ways. The functions that can be measured are detection, delay, and response. Detection is measured by the probability of detection as well as time for communication and assessment.[61] The frequency of nuisance alarms is also a performance measure of the detection function.

Delay is measured by the time it takes to defeat an obstacle. Response to alarms can be measured in several ways, including the probability of accurate communication to the response force; time to communicate; probability of deployment to adversary location; time to deploy; and the effectiveness of the response force.[62]

Building Your Facility

If you are constructing a new facility, you should take security into consideration in designing your facility.

1. Exterior walls should be built with the most durable materials such as stone, brick, or masonry.[63]
2. Provide security entry points with metal-clad or solid-core exterior doors.[64]
3. Ground-level windows and windows in exterior doors should have secure panes, such as wire glass, tempered glass, laminated glass, or plastic laminates.[65]
4. Molded hinges should be installed on exterior doors to prevent tampering.[66]
5. Eliminate all but the essential doors and windows.[67]
6. Include provisions for the disabled, children, and the elderly.
7. Ensure specific fire-resistant material is installed through the interior.[68]
8. Points of possible access or escape that breach the exterior of the building or the perimeter—such as skylights, air-conditioning vents, sewer ducts, manholes, or any opening larger than 96 in^2—should be protected.[69]

Final Thoughts

There are several things to keep in mind when choosing physical security measures.

1. Start with what you have and add other people, technologies, and processes as needed.
2. Think about the compatibility of technologies, processes, and people.
3. Technology is ineffective without people who are trained and who use it properly.
4. Technology can both create as well as reduce vulnerability to disasters.[70]

While it may seem overwhelming at first to create a physical protection system, if you follow the steps outlined in this chapter as well as Chapter 4 on evaluating risk, the process will be easier. As always, consult with professionals to ensure the system meets your needs. Do not be drawn in by flashy sales presentations that promise what they can't deliver or that try to tell you how to protect your facility without knowing anything about it. The next chapter will show you ways to create a secure environment without turning your facility into a maximum security prison.

End Notes

1. Roper C. A., *Risk Management for Security Professionals* (Boston: Butterworth-Heinemann, 1999), 14.
2. Ibid.
3. Garcia M. L., *The Design and Evaluation of Physical Protection Systems*, Second Edition (Boston: Butterworth-Heinemann, 2008).

4. Ibid.
5. Ibid.
6. Ibid.
7. Ibid, p. 6.
8. See note 3 above.
9. See note 3 above, p. 7.
10. Ibid.
11. See note 3 above.
12. See note 3 above.
13. See note 9 above.
14. See note 3 above.
15. See note 9 above.
16. See note 9 above.
17. See note 3 above, p. 8.
18. Patterson D. G., *Implementing Physical Protection Systems: A Practical Guide* (Alexandria: ASIS International, 2004).
19. See note 3 above.
20. See note 3 above.
21. See note 3 above.
22. See note 3 above.
23. See note 3 above.
24. See note 3 above.
25. See note 3 above.
26. McCrie R. D., *Security Operations Management*, Second Edition (Boston: Butterworth-Heinemann, 2007).
27. See note 3 above.
28. See note 3 above.
29. See note 3 above, p. 113.
30. See note 3 above.
31. See note 3 above.
32. See note 3 above.
33. See note 3 above.
34. See note 3 above.
35. See note 3 above.
36. See note 3 above.
37. See note 3 above.
38. See note 3 above.
39. See note 3 above.
40. See note 3 above.
41. Fischer R. J., Halibozek E. and Green G, *Introduction to Security*, Eighth Edition (Massachusetts: Butterworth-Heinemann, 2008).
42. Ibid.
43. See note 3 above.
44. See note 3 above.
45. See note 45 above, p. 209.
46. See note 3 above.
47. See note 3 above.
48. See note 3 above, p. 211.
49. See note 3 above.
50. See note 3 above.

51. See note 3 above.
52. See note 3 above.
53. See note 3 above.
54. See note 3 above.
55. See note 41 above.
56. See note 41 above.
57. See note 41 above.
58. See note 41 above.
59. Tyska L. A. and Fennelly L.J, *Physical Security: 150 Things You should Know* (Massachusetts: Butterworth-Heinemann, 2000).
60. Ibid.
61. See note 3 above.
62. See note 3 above.
63. Welch R. H., *Serving by Safeguarding Your Church* (Grand Rapids: Zondervan Press, 2002).
64. Ibid.
65. Ibid.
66. Ibid.
67. See note 59 above.
68. See note 59 above.
69. See note 41 above.
70. Alexander D., *Principles of Emergency Planning and Management* (New York: Oxford University Press, 2002).

Utilizing the Total Environment

As mentioned in Chapter 3, environmental security and the closely related concepts of crime prevention through environmental design (CPTED) and crime prevention through opportunity reduction can be some of the easiest ways to make your facility safe and secure while still maintaining a welcoming atmosphere. This chapter will explain the basic concepts and provide ways that you can use them in your facility.

Unless you are designing your facility from the ground up, there are some limitations as to what you can do. However, the principles of CPTED focus on the use of space to create security and do not necessarily require renovation or reconstruction of an existing facility. This can make the use of CPTED principles one of the more cost-effective security methods in that you use what you have instead of buying multitudes of fancy technology and equipment.

The benefit of CPTED and similar methodologies is the focus on the total environment, including the facility, grounds, parking lot, neighboring businesses, and the surrounding community. Therefore, security is not isolated to the perimeter or interior of the building but takes into account sidewalks, parking areas, street traffic, and other adjacent areas. This holistic approach is important to security as a whole because it integrates people, processes, and technology into a complete system.

Benefits of CPTED

1. Creates a more welcoming atmosphere for legitimate users
2. Can be cost-effective
3. Can be aesthetically pleasing
4. Looks at the property as a whole
5. Reduces opportunities for criminal activity
6. Valuable for designing and managing exterior as well as interior spaces[1]
7. Can be used in planning stages or in facilities that are already built
8. Treatment of crime problems at various environmental scales[2]
9. Integration of prevention approaches[3]
10. Identification of short-term and long-term goals[4]
11. Encouragement of collective responses to problems[5]
12. Interdisciplinary approach to urban problems[6]
13. Encouragement of better police/community relations[7]
14. Development of security guidelines and standards[8]
15. Assistance in urban revitalization[9]
16. Acquisition of development funds[10]
17. Institutionalization of crime-prevention policies and practices[11]

Randall Atlas perfectly summarizes this first point as "the emphasis in CPTED design falls on the design and use of space, a practice that deviates from the traditional target-hardening approach."[12] In a typical target-hardening approach, there would be bars on the windows, metal detectors at each entry point, and armed guards roaming the halls. Though this would certainly protect your facility, it would also cause your attendees tremendous fear and anxiety, and they would likely find a new institution to attend.

What is CPTED?

Crime prevention through environmental design is based on the idea that most crimes are committed as a result of opportunity wherein criminals seek the easiest targets such as unlocked car doors, inadequate nighttime parking lot lighting, areas with multiple places for concealment, or a person who is not paying attention to their surroundings and so can be easily robbed. CPTED counters this by reducing the opportunities for criminal activity and by using environmental cues to influence behavior in different ways. Legitimate users of space will feel secure while illegitimate users, i.e., criminals, will feel at greater risk of detection or apprehension.[13]

CPTED has a deterrent effect on potential adversaries in the following ways.[14]

- Target access is made impossible, too difficult, or too time-consuming.
- Concealment places are eliminated, thereby increasing the likelihood of detection.
- The likelihood of the arrival of security or law enforcement while the offender is still on the premises is increased.
- The likelihood of the offender's successful escape is decreased due to poor escape routes and probable interception.
- Increased observation opportunities increase the probability that the offender will be identified.

CPTED Approaches and Measures

There are two basic approaches—passive and active—with CPTED.[15] Active approaches include patrols, alarm systems, intrusion detection systems, CCTV, and communication devices. Passive approaches are design features such as lighting, landscaping, and natural surveillance elements.

CPTED measures can also be classified as organized, mechanical, and natural.

Organized approaches are labor-intensive and require the use of people for protection such as paid armed and unarmed security officers. These personnel costs are in addition to the standard human resource costs of human activities.[16] They also include police officer patrols, security teams, and neighborhood watches. These strategies use people with the ability to observe, report, and intervene.[17]

Mechanical approaches are capital-intensive and involve hardware and technology such as fences, bollards, CCTV systems, alarms, and locks.[18] These measures should be used in conjunction with people and design strategies. Technology only works if monitored properly.

Natural approaches can be the least capital-intensive and labor-intensive. The premise is that a natural approach factors behavior management into what was going to be done anyway. These approaches should be maximized first before trying other methods. They also make operational and mechanical approaches work more efficiently and reduce the extra costs of organized and mechanical security.[19]

CPTED Concepts

To use CPTED effectively, we need to define a few concepts.

1. Environment: includes people and their physical and social surroundings[20]
2. Design: includes physical, social, management, and law enforcement directives that seek to positively affect human behavior as people interact with the environment[21]
3. Natural: deriving access control and surveillance as a byproduct of the normal and routine use of the environment[22]
4. Defensible space: the idea that crime flourishes because design prevents owners from exercising informal control over their environment[23]
   a. Territorial definition: use of real or symbolic barriers to encourage owners to adopt proprietary or territorial attitudes[24]
   b. Visibility and surveillance: allows people to see what is happening
   c. Stigmatization: effective use of materials, good architectural design, and good structural planning to prevent a facility from seeming vulnerable[25]
   d. Adjacent areas: security of adjoining areas partly determined by the strategic location of intensively used communal areas[26]

Defensible space creates the appearance of a community that "defends" itself.[27] Ways to accomplish this are the creation of new on-site facilities such as playgrounds and day care centers and the renovation of existing facilities.

Symbolic barriers "define areas or relate them to particular buildings without physically preventing intrusion."[28] These include hedges, low walls, open fencing, and signage. However, the effectiveness of symbolic barriers is affected by the following:

1. The capacity of adversaries to read and understand symbols[29]
2. The capacity of users to maintain controls and reinforce space definition as symbolically defined[30]
3. The capacity of the defined space to require the adversary to make their intentions obvious[31]
4. The capacity of users to challenge the presence of an adversary and to take subsequent action[32]

Behavior Management

CPTED affects the behavior of users in important ways. Space affects normal and abnormal users as "the further one is from a potential threat, the easier that threat is to manage."[33] It increases the space, and therefore the choices, that normal users have, whereas decreasing the space and choices for the abnormal users.[34] It makes the abnormal user, i.e., criminal, feel at greater risk for detection or detention, while normal users feel safe.[35]

Rational potential offenders are concerned with the ease of entering an area; how visible, attractive, or vulnerable the targets appear; the chances of being seen; if seen, will people do anything about it; and if there is a quick direct route for leaving the site after committing a crime.[36] Therefore, CPTED strategies are meant to counter these concerns, thereby decreasing the likelihood of criminal activity. Proper management of space and human resources "increases supervision and control, thus decreasing opportunity for abnormal behavior or undesired activities."[37]

Aesthetics and appearance such as horticulture, color, and light positively enhance behavior management as well.[38] Bright open spaces increase the chances for surveillance. Plants, flowers, and shrubs can define territory. Well-managed landscaping also contributes to the concepts of defensible space and territoriality. However, one must take care that landscaping elements do not provide hiding places for potential criminals or obstruct the surveillance by legitimate users.

Space Assessment 3-D Approach

To assess the environment for CPTED improvements, you need data on local crimes, community demographics, land use, observations, and user or resident input.[39] The assessment focuses on three areas: designation, definition, and design. Each area should be evaluated by asking the following questions as outlined in Crowe and Fennelly.[40]

Designation Questions[41]

- What is the designated purpose of the space?
- What was it originally intended to be used for?
- How well does the space support its current use?
- How well does the space support its intended use?
- Is there conflict?

Definition Questions[42]

- How is the space defined?
- Is it clear who owns it?
- Where are its borders?
- Are there social or cultural definitions that affect how that space is used?
- Are the legal or administrative rules clearly set out and reinforced in policy?
- Are there signs?
- Is there conflict or confusion between the space's designated purpose and its definition?

Design Questions[43]

- How well does the physical design support the intended function?
- How well does the physical design support the definition of the desired or accepted behaviors?
- Does the physical design conflict with or impede the productive use of the space or the proper functioning of the intended human activity?
- Is there confusion or conflict in terms of the manner in which the physical design is intended to control behavior?

Putting CPTED Principles to Work

Once the space has been assessed, it is time to apply the principles of CPTED to your facility.

1. Provide clear border definition of controlled space, either symbolically or physically.[44] This can be accomplished through sidewalks, fences, perimeter landscaping, and signage.
2. Provide clearly marked transitional zones that indicate movement from public to semipublic to private space.[45] Elements that define borders also mark transitions to private property.
3. Territorial reinforcement can be achieved through clear border definition and transitional zones.
4. Relocate gathering areas to locations with natural surveillance and access control or to locations away from the view of would-be offenders.[46]
5. Place safe activities in unsafe locations to bring along the natural surveillance of these activities and to increase the perception of safety for normal users and of risk to offenders.[47] Safe activities draw legitimate users who exhibit challenging or controlling behaviors that tell abnormal users they are at greater risk of scrutiny or intervention. Use caution when adopting this strategy as you want to reduce vulnerability not increase it.
6. Place unsafe activities in safe spots to overcome the vulnerability of these activities with the natural surveillance and access control of the safe area.[48] Locating these activities near windows of occupied space or within tightly controlled areas increases the chance of observation.
7. Redesignate the use of space to provide natural barriers to conflicting activities.[49] The threat does not have to be real to create the perception of risk for desired users.
8. Improve scheduling of space to increase the perception or reality of natural surveillance.[50] In other words, reduce the times when the facility is unoccupied.
9. Redesign space to increase the perception or reality of natural surveillance.[51] The presence of CCTV cameras increases the perception and reality of surveillance, whereas hidden cameras only increase the reality of it and do not alter behavior.
10. Overcome distance and isolation through improved communication and design efficiencies.[52] The use of public address systems, cell phones, or walkie-talkies enables communication across distances.
11. Increase natural surveillance by ensuring windows are on each side of the building and that they provide unobstructed views of all areas of the grounds including sidewalks and parking areas.
12. Increase natural access control through natural spatial definition.[53]
13. One-way streets, gates, and speed bumps control vehicle traffic to reduce nonresident through access.[54]
14. Parking areas should be open with good lighting and away from places where adversaries could hide.
15. Locking some exterior doors funnels users through specific areas, thereby reducing the number of ways adversaries can access a building.
16. Support the organization's activities by using programs that involve legitimate users "to discourage offenders, enhance crime prevention awareness, increase community involvement, and provide social services."[55]
17. Maintenance of landscaping elements, repair of broken or damaged physical elements, and keeping areas neat and clean—including application of fresh paint or power washing exterior walls—show that users care about the facility and reducing its vulnerability to illegitimate users.

> **Nine Major CPTED Strategies**
>
> 1. Provide a clear border definition of controlled space.
> 2. Clearly mark transition zones.
> 3. Relocate gathering areas.
> 4. Locate safe activities in unsafe locations.
> 5. Locate unsafe activities in safe locations.
> 6. Redesignate the use of space to provide natural barriers.
> 7. Improve scheduling of space.
> 8. Redesign space to increase natural surveillance.
> 9. Overcome distance and isolation.

Final Thoughts

Security should not interfere with the mission of the facility. A careful design and use of physical space is concerned with the purpose of the space and influencing human decisions and behavior.[56] The principles and strategies of CPTED are a practical way to harden the target. Traditional target-hardening approaches often lead to constraints on use, access, and enjoyment of the hardened environment.[57] This is in contrast with CPTED, whose "underlying objective is to help the various disciplines do a better job of achieving their primary objectives, with the added byproduct of improved security and loss prevention."[58]

End Notes

1. Crowe T. D. and Fennelly L. J., *Crime Prevention through Environmental Design*, Third Edition (Boston: Butterworth-Heinemann, 2013).
2. Ibid.
3. Ibid.
4. Ibid.
5. Ibid.
6. Ibid.
7. Ibid.
8. Ibid.
9. Ibid.
10. Ibid.
11. Ibid.
12. Atlas R. (2013), p. 25.
13. See note 1 above.
14. Quarles C. L. and Ratliff P. L., *Crime Prevention for Houses of Worship* (Alexandria: American Society for Industrial Security, 2001).
15. Ibid.
16. See note 1 above.
17. Atlas R. I., *21st Century Security and CPTED: Designing for Criminal Infrastructure and Crime Prevention*, Second Edition (Boca Raton: CRC Press, 2013).

18. See note 1 above.
19. See note 1 above.
20. See note 1 above.
21. See note 1 above.
22. See note 1 above.
23. See note 1 above.
24. See note 1 above.
25. See note 1 above.
26. See note 1 above.
27. Tyska L. A. and Fennelly L. J., *Physical Security: 150 Things You Should Know* (Massachusetts: Butterworth-Heinemann, 2000).
28. Ibid, p. 53.
29. See note 27 above.
30. See note 27 above.
31. See note 27 above.
32. See note 27 above.
33. See note 1 above, p. 17.
34. See note 1 above.
35. See note 1 above.
36. See note 17 above.
37. See note 1 above, p. 18.
38. See note 1 above.
39. See note 1 above.
40. See note 1 above.
41. See note 1 above, p. 30.
42. See note 1 above, p. 30–31.
43. See note 1 above, p. 31.
44. See note 1 above.
45. See note 1 above.
46. See note 1 above.
47. See note 1 above.
48. See note 1 above.
49. See note 1 above.
50. See note 1 above.
51. See note 1 above.
52. See note 1 above.
53. See note 1 above.
54. See note 1 above.
55. See note 27 above, p. 49
56. See note 1 above.
57. See note 1 above, p. 26.
58. See note 1 above, p. 56.

Developing Policies and Procedures   7

Planning is one of the most important things you can do to secure your facility. Your security plan should involve developing policies and procedures to handle the risks identified in your risk assessment. Policies and procedures explain certain aspects of operations, outline steps to be taken in the event a particular situation occurs, and state consequences for failure to comply with these established processes. Policies and their enforcement should be logical, realistic, and consistent.

Almost every organization has plans for what to do in case of a fire or other natural disaster, so it makes sense to be prepared for human-caused emergencies as well. Being prepared for an event has several distinct advantages.

1. Instructs people on their roles and responsibilities
2. Contributes to consistency in performance, which increases efficiency[1]
3. Describes specific actions for handling specific incidents
4. Provides liability protection if properly developed and followed
5. Reduces decision-making time as employees know how they are supposed to respond or proceed in a given situation
6. Enhances management control and provides for objective performance evaluation[2]

A policy is a written statement of management's position or direction regarding an issue.[3] Basically, it is a statement of what management wants. Policies establish strategic objectives and priorities for the organization and identify those who are primarily accountable for them.[4] They also outline the tasks, responsibilities, and expectations for employees and volunteers based on their roles in the organization.

Procedures are the detailed steps employees must follow in order to achieve the desired results.[5] For every policy that is written, there should be a corresponding set of procedures to accompany it. Often presented as forms or chronological lists of steps to be taken, they are detailed implementation instructions for staff and volunteers.[6] They can be used for corrective action of inappropriate behavior or underperformance. To be effective, they must be communicated to those who are expected to follow them. Chapter 15 will cover implementation and training. While policies change infrequently, the procedures to address them may change more often as they are evaluated and improved in reaction to changing demands, conditions, and needs.

Policies and procedures should be established for all aspects of business. This includes guidelines for employees, ushers, greeters, volunteers, and team members. Strict procedures should be adopted for those dealing with children and money as they are two of the most vulnerable areas in the facility. Emergency response plans are also necessary as the effects of natural disasters can be as devastating as a violent crime.

Policies and procedures should have the following elements:

1. Organized in a logical sequence
2. Clear and easy to follow

3. Complete, but not overly detailed
4. Contain a glossary defining any terms used[7]
5. Assign responsibility for planning to individuals within the organization and describe the emergency lines of authority[8]
6. Outline specific resources and tasks required to carry out operations
7. Flexible and adaptable enough to address unforeseen events
8. Contain references to other plans or documents
9. State assumptions upon which the plan is based or by which it is constrained[9]
10. Date created, effective date, and subsequent revision dates
11. Distribution list[10]

You can follow the format of your emergency preparedness policies and procedures or you can use the basic format below. The length of the policy does not matter so long as they are complete. Use a consistent format for writing your policies and procedures.

1. Title
2. Purpose
3. Scope
4. Objectives
5. Situation and assumptions upon which it is based[11]
6. Concept of operations describing the overall strategy or approach[12]
7. Organization and assignment of responsibilities
8. Administration, resources, and logistics
9. Plan development and maintenance
10. Activation and implementation
11. Training
12. Exercises
13. Authorities and references
14. Blank forms, checklists, contracts, and other documents[13]

Topics for Policies and Procedures

There are many topics that can be established including the following:

1. General
   a. Reporting, auditing, and review arrangements[14]
   b. Training type, duration, or topics to be covered
   c. Development, disbursement, implementation, training, evaluation, and update of policies and procedures
   d. Access control
   e. Ethics and code of conduct
   f. Public relations
2. People
   a. Hiring
   b. Use of volunteers
   c. Money-handling
   d. Access control management
   e. Prohibited items and substances
   f. Accounts payable and receivable[15]

3. Situations
   a. Lockdown or shelter-in-place[16]
   b. Reporting crimes and/or suspicious behavior
   c. Internal communication and notifications
   d. Threat response and abatement[17]
   e. Contacting emergency responders
   f. Crowd control
   g. Traffic control
   h. Church vehicle accidents
   i. Personal injury
   j. Protection of employees working alone[18]
4. Property
   a. Facility usage
   b. Identifying and managing suspicious packages
   c. Safeguarding employer property
   d. Acceptable personal use of employer assets such as computers, phones, or office equipment
   e. Investigations
   f. Property inventory, control, marking, and disposal[19]
   g. Key control and accountability
   h. Vehicle access control
   i. Regulatory compliance
5. Information
   a. Disclosure of proprietary information[20]
   b. Information handling, including marking, storage, transmission, disposal, and destruction[21]
6. Activities
   a. Day care
   b. Off-site trips
   c. Counseling
   d. Overnight trips
   e. Sleepovers

The preceding represent just a few. Look at the results of your risk assessment to develop policies and procedures that are appropriate and relevant for your facility. Look at the activities conducted at your facility and the types of services provided to identify other areas that need policies and procedures developed.

Emergency Plans for Security Incidents

Although a continuous process of often overlapping phases, a comprehensive emergency management plan is typically divided into the pre-event activities of preparedness and mitigation and post-event activities of response and recovery.[22]

Alert procedures, warning processes, and evacuation procedures are necessary components of emergency preparedness. The warning process entails a combination of technical and social measures involving "adequate knowledge of impending threats, a means of disseminating instructions, and reasonable certainty that these will be understood and acted upon."[23] Warnings should give recipients enough time to react, but not so much time that precautions or credibility lapse.[24] They should also clearly explain what actions need to be taken to prepare for an incident and should be repeated with each message that follows detailing changes in the hazard, the impact, and the required response.[25]

Evacuation plans are of particular importance, whether the crisis is natural or caused by humans.[26] A major issue is the custodial problem.[27] Contacting parents and/or legal guardians may be difficult, and individuals may be unable to leave the institution. In such situations, staff may have to stay late to take care of the children until parents or rescue personnel arrive. The religious institution itself may become a shelter

In addition, staff may have children of their own to check on. Cooperation of parents with emergency plans is of the utmost importance.[28] Procedures must be in place to keep track of when, where, and to whom each child was released after evacuation.[29] The facility must have a parent–child reunification policy and set of procedures.

Special considerations must be made concerning disabled persons and the elderly. This includes communication, evacuation, shelter-in-place, and reunion with their next of kin. It is probably best to leave the evacuation of nonambulatory persons to professional emergency personnel.[30]

Of equal importance is the cooperation between staff and emergency workers.[31] Emergency plans should be tested at regular intervals to ensure that the staff know what to do and to identify any problems or weaknesses in the plan.[32] It is vital that staff know how to maintain processes or how to shut them down when disaster strikes.[33] A comprehensive emergency plan should take into account vulnerabilities, risks, and impact.

Recovery Plans

Recovery plans from an incident should be developed as well. Chapter 11 details considerations for recovering from an event.

Recovery includes both short-term and long-term issues. Many of these issues can be addressed in the emergency plan. However, some issues will not be revealed until sometime after the incident has occurred.

Responsibilities and activities should be prioritized. Consider including critical incidence stress management services as a vital component of employee assistance programs as mental health professionals and counselors are needed to address the mental health and well-being of victims in the aftermath of a catastrophic event.[34] The plans should contain site-specific information including building floor plans, primary and secondary evacuation routes, designated meeting sites, exits, and locations of alarms, telephones, and first aid kits.

An important component of short-term recovery includes protection against a continuing threat and a search for secondary threats.[35] Actions should be delineated to deal with the discovery of secondary threats and a method for continually assessing the total situation.[36]

Following development of the plan and acceptance by leaders, training of plan requirements should be conducted with all employees and volunteers. Periodic evacuation drills should also be conducted, critiqued, and evaluated.

Information Security Policies

Every activity performed in an organization is reliant on some type of information. The most important aspect of information security is to involve all employees and volunteers. They must incorporate security into their standard operating procedures, be made aware of their responsibilities, and be held accountable for security. As it has often been said "a network is only as secure as the weakest point."[37]

The key to a successful information security program is a continuous process of evaluation and adaptation. The first step is a baseline assessment of the current state of the information security program.[38] The second step is the evaluation process, which involves identifying and prioritizing risks that will be addressed with specific plans so improvements can be made.[39] The final step involves continually reevaluating priorities as you respond to normal operations as well as tactical issues.[40] Reminiscent of the disaster management cycle, it takes into account the ever-changing needs of preparedness and the continuous reevaluation of threats, vulnerabilities, and plans.

Everything an organization does involves information of some type, whether oral, written, or printed. Regardless of form, information should be marked, distributed, copied, mailed, transported, stored, and destroyed in accordance with established procedures.[41]

Information security and cybersecurity are more than installing antivirus software and firewalls on your computer, although that is a good place to start. The ease of accessibility to information also makes it more vulnerable to compromise.

There are several types of policies that can be written including the following:

1. Account administration: who gets access to what and how it is decided[42]
2. Remote access: email or other access when not in the office[43]
3. Vulnerability management: holes that someone can use to attack your organization[44]
4. Acceptable use policies: guidelines that define appropriate and inappropriate use of data and information systems[45]
5. Security awareness
6. Information handling
7. Clean desk policy
8. Information distribution
9. Emergency response
10. Online presence

They can be written as individual policies or incorporated into one general policy that guides the daily operations of the business.

Types of Information to Be Protected

The following is a partial list of the types of information that need to be protected.

1. Full names and addresses of members/attendees
2. Amount of money collected via donations, fundraisers, charity events, etc.
3. Security equipment
4. Passwords
5. Keys

Enterprise Information Security Policy

An enterprise information security policy (EISP) is the general security policy for an organization. It serves to set the strategic direction, scope, and tone for all of an organization's information security efforts by assigning responsibilities and guiding the development, implementation, and management requirements of the program.[46]

There are four main aspects of security to consider in the EISP: physical, operations, communications, and network.[47] As discussed in Chapter 5, physical includes fences, locks, security cameras, and other countermeasures. Operations are the policies and procedures that govern aspects of information security. Communications involve guidelines on cell phone usage as well as software protection of internet and email. Network security involves virtual private networks (VPN) and backup servers.

The main components of an EISP are as follows:[48]

1. Statement of purpose
2. IT security elements
3. Need for IT security
4. IT security roles and responsibilities
5. Reference to other IT standards and guidelines

The policy should specify how information is protected, used, handled, accessed, disseminated, and destroyed.[49] It should also include data and program damage disclaimers, legal conflicts, any exceptions to the policy, and conformance to industry-specific information security standards.[50]

Figure 7.1 defines the key areas to protect according to Lineman and lists how they can be protected.[51]

Sample Policies

Some examples of security measures are discussed in the following sections. They are meant to be a guide and should be adapted to your specific facility. Small religious institutions probably do not have an intranet or email addresses specifically for the facility. However, examples of those policies are included.

Computers
1. Employees are assigned a username and required to change their password every 60 days.
2. All computers prohibit the downloading and installation of programs unless performed by IT personnel.
3. Firewalls, antivirus software, intrusion detection software, and fraud monitoring web browsers are installed on each unit.
4. Employees are prohibited from downloading files and must get special permission to use devices that plug into a USB port such as flash drives and iPods.
5. Computers are also to be locked (CTRL-ALT-DEL) when the user leaves their desk.

Internet
1. The Internet must be accessible to all employees.
2. Computers are protected through the use of firewalls, antivirus software, intrusion detection software, fraud monitoring browsers, and absence of adware or spyware programs.

Key Areas	Method of Protection
Desktop and personal data security	• Individual computers are password-protected for each individual user. • Programs cannot be installed by individual users, only by IT personnel.
Secure web browsing	• Firewalls • Software that detects and destroys spyware, adware, and other malware. • Use only browser and connection provided by employer.
Email and instant messaging security	• Instant messaging is prohibited. • Email is secured.
Handling confidential information	• Classification of documents. • Proper disposal of what is no longer needed.
Managing passwords	• Passwords must be a combination of uppercase and lowercase letters, numbers, and symbols. • They must be changed every 60 days.
Physical security	• Cell phones, PDAs, and laptops are prohibited for all visitors. • Duress alarms. • Break-resistant glass on all doors and windows. • Security cameras that monitor inside the building and the outside perimeter.
Data backup and disposal	• Data is constantly saved and backed up on several servers. • Virtual Private Network.
Protecting customer privacy	• Disclosure policy based on document classification system.
Compliance with laws and regulations	• Compliance officer who ensures following of State and Federal guidelines as required.
Your right to privacy	• Disclosure policy based on document classification system.

Figure 7.1 Key IT areas to protect and how to protect them.

3. As previously stated, non-work related files are prohibited from being downloaded onto the computer system.

Intranet

1. Data is stored on a Virtual Private Network through a proxy server that protects the main servers.
2. Data is constantly backed up. Remote access to certain applications in the Intranet is possible through a password only.
3. The intranet is on a separate server from the Website.

Email

1. Work email has a high spam filter that also quarantines attachments.
2. Individuals must speak with IT personnel to allow attachments to go through.

Telephones

1. Cell phone usage is prohibited by employees and visitors alike in the buildings.
2. Visitors must either lock their phone in their car or turn it into the access control officer at the front desk.
3. Employees may have their cell phones and PDAs, but must have them turned off while in the facilities.

Face-to-Face Meetings

1. Face-to-face business is always conducted at the facility.
2. Under no circumstances should proprietary information be discussed in public where others can overhear.

Clean Desk Policy

1. Lock PCs when not in use.
2. Lock personally identifiable materials away when not in use or when away from desk.
3. Do not leave desk or office keys hidden or unattended.
4. Shred unneeded materials.

Issue-Specific Security Policies

Issue-specific security polices (ISSP) provide "detailed, targeted guidance to instruct all members of the organization in the use of a process, technology, or system that is used by the organization."[52]

Email Use

1. An employee's business email address is to be used primarily for business use. Some personal use is allowed. However, signing up for non-work related newsletters is strictly prohibited.
2. Personal email sites such as Yahoo, AOL, Hotmail, and Gmail are also prohibited and will not be accessible.

Internet and Web Use

1. Internet and Web usage is primarily for business.
2. Personal use is allowed during lunch.
3. Downloading programs, software, or other files is strictly prohibited.

Policy Distribution

Once the plans, policies, and procedures have been written, they need to be continually tested, evaluated, revised, and updated to account for changes in risk, vulnerability, resources, and other elements that impact their effectiveness. A good plan is useless unless it is given to the proper individuals to implement it. Therefore, another component of the plan should include arrangements for testing, disseminating, and updating it.[53] Plan distribution and publicity, the conducting and evaluating of field exercises, and the standard or automatic procedures for updating the plan should also be devised.[54]

Once the policy is written and approved by management, it must be distributed to employees. Policies are not simply distributed with the hopes that employees read and understand them. Security is everyone's business, so it is important to develop a comprehensive training program to ensure that all employees are aware of their roles and responsibilities in protecting information.

When a new policy is written or an existing one is updated, employees should be notified of the change, what has been changed, and why the change was made. They should also receive a copy of the policy so they can view it for themselves.

Web-based surveys and quizzes can be periodically given to test employee understanding of security policies. Scenario training can test comprehension and application of policy. In addition, incentives such as contests and prizes can be instituted at random intervals to encourage continued study. All employees should sign an acknowledgment that they have read and understood the policy. This should be maintained in their personnel file.

Final Thoughts

Policies and procedures are essential to securing your facility. Establishing them is one of the most cost-effective security countermeasures you can institute. They take into account the importance of people in risk management. It does not matter how advanced your technology is if people do not use it properly.

When people do not know how to respond in a given situation, they may inadvertently compromise security. They may also become paralyzed with indecision, thereby putting themselves at greater risk.

It is wise to have legal counsel review your policies and procedures to ensure they do not conflict with laws and regulations. They may also be able to suggest recommendations for reducing liability as well as risk. Their advice can also protect you from discrimination lawsuits. In addition, you want to evaluate whether your policies are relevant to your mission. They must take into account the organizational culture and the atmosphere you are trying to promote.

End Notes

1. Sennewald C. A., *Effective Security Management*, Fourth Edition (Boston: Butterworth-Heinemann, 2003).
2. Ibid.
3. Ibid.
4. Broder J. F. and Tucker E. *Risk Analysis and the Security Survey*, Fourth Edition (Boston: Elsevier Butterworth Heinemann, 2012).
5. See note 1 above.
6. See note 4 above.
7. See note 4 above.
8. See note 4 above.
9. See note 4 above.
10. See note 4 above.
11. See note 4 above.
12. See note 4 above.
13. See note 4 above.
14. See note 4 above.
15. See note 4 above.
16. American Crime Prevention Institute, *Church Crime Prevention* (2008). Retrieved from http://www.santarosa.fl.gov/coad/documents/ChurchCrimePreventionVSept2008.pdf.

17. Ibid.
18. See note 4 above.
19. See note 4 above.
20. See note 4 above.
21. See note 4 above.
22. McGlown K. J. *Terrorism and Disaster Management: Preparing Healthcare Leaders for the New Reality* (Chicago: Health Administration Press, 2004).
23. Alexander D. *Principles of Emergency Planning and Management* (New York: Oxford University Press, 2002), 146.
24. Alexander D. *Principles of Emergency Planning and Management* (New York: Oxford University Press, 2002).
25. Ibid.
26. Ibid.
27. Ibid.
28. Ibid.
29. Ibid.
30. Carcara W. S., *Advising Houses of Worship on a Comprehensive and Balanced Security Plan* (2009). Retrieved from www.policechiefmagazine.org/magazine/index.cfm?fuseaction=display_arch&article_id=1845&issue_id=72009.
31. See note 24 above.
32. See note 24 above.
33. See note 24 above.
34. Maiden R. P., Paul R., and Thompson C. eds., *Workplace Disaster, Preparedness, Response, and Management* (Haworth Press, 2006).
35. See note 24 above.
36. See note 24 above.
37. Lineman D. J., *Information Protection Made Easy: A Guide for Employees and Contractors* (Houston: Information Shield, 2006), 7.
38. Egan M., *The Executive Guide to Information Security: Threats, Challenges, and Solutions* (Indianapolis: Addison-Wesley, 2005).
39. Ibid.
40. Ibid.
41. Fay J. J., *Contemporary Security Management*, Second Edition (Boston: Butterworth-Heinemann, 2006).
42. See note 38 above.
43. See note 38 above.
44. See note 38 above.
45. See note 38 above.
46. Whitman M. E. and Mattord H. J., *Management of Information Security*, Second Edition (Boston: Thomson Course Technology, 2010).
47. Ibid.
48. Ibid.
49. Ibid.
50. Ibid.
51. Lineman D. J., *Information Protection Made Easy: A Guide for Employees and Contractors* (Houston: Information Shield, 2006).
52. See note 46 above, p. 118.
53. See note 24 above.
54. See note 24 above.

Identifying and Handling At-Risk People

Many religious institutions provide services to disadvantaged groups through outreach programs. These can include charitable services to individuals and groups such as the homeless, mentally ill, victims of crime or natural disasters, reformed criminals, substance abusers, and many other types of people. Many people who have had difficulties seek help from local religious institutions. There are several ways to aid those less fortunate without endangering employees, volunteers, and members of the religious institution. Some of these services include food drives, bill paying, counseling services, etc.

According to the National Victim Assistance Academy, certain activities are common in organizations that have experienced violence.[1] These include characteristics that are common to religious institutions including the following:

1. Contact with the public
2. Exchange of money
3. Working with unstable persons
4. Working alone or in small numbers
5. Working at night or late hours
6. Working in a high-crime area
7. Working in a community-based setting

Places that do not have strong security measures are also common targets.

Although staff can learn to recognize at-risk individuals, certain behaviors require intervention by professionals to ensure they receive the help and support that they need. These include the following:

- Severe aggression and/or behavior issues
- Chemical dependency and abuse
- Domestic violence
- Suicidal tendencies
- Mental health issues

In these cases, individuals should be referred to outside assistance programs. Staff is not expected to be able to handle these issues on their own, but they can provide resources to help individuals seeking professional assistance.

Simply providing support and contact information for professional services may be the only avenues available to staff. Nevertheless, they are important steps in ensuring the health, safety, and welfare of all involved.

Support services can be provided to all even if no one is identified as at-risk. Simply letting people know what resources are available and how to contact them can provide help. Some may feel comfortable accepting help only if they can do so without anyone at the religious institution knowing about it. Assure staff and attendees of confidentiality and enforce it.

One of the most effective ways to gauge potential danger in dealing with an individual is to conduct a threat assessment.

Threat Assessment

Not all threats are the same, but all threats should be evaluated in a timely manner with decisions regarding how they are handled made quickly. A one-size-fits-all approach does not work. Some threats can indicate a clear and present danger, whereas others represent little or no real threat to anyone's safety. However, no threat should be ignored. They should be evaluated with a threat assessment.

Threat assessments seek to make an informed judgment based on two questions:[2]

1. How credible and serious is the threat itself?
2. To what extent does the person threatening appear to have the resources, intent, and motivation to carry out the threat?

Spoken, written, or symbolic, "a threat is an expression of the intent to do harm or act out violently against someone or something."[3] Symbolic threats include motioning with one's hands as though shooting another or slitting their throat.

Threats can be classified into four categories: direct, indirect, veiled, and conditional.[4]

A direct threat is very specific, clear, explicit, and straightforward, such as "I'm going to put a bomb at the front entrance of the mosque." An indirect threat is just the opposite. In an indirect threat, violence is implied as something that could but not necessarily will occur, such as "If I wanted to, I could take out everyone in this church."

A veiled threat strongly implies but does not explicitly threaten violence, leaving it to "the potential victim(s) to interpret the message and give a definitive meaning to the threat."[5] Statements include "We would be better off without churches around" or "a particular religion shouldn't exist anymore." The potential for violence is there, but there are no specifics.

A conditional threat is often seen in extortion cases and warns of violence that will happen unless certain demands or terms are met.

Regardless of the type of threat received, they should be taken very seriously. However, there are certain factors that indicate an increased likelihood that the threat will be carried out. These include the following:[6]

1. Specific and plausible details
2. Emotional content
3. Precipitating stressors
4. Predisposing factors

Details include the identity of the victim(s); the reason for making the threat; the means, weapon, and method by which it is to be carried out; the date, time, and place where it will occur; and concrete information about plans or preparations that already have been made such as "I have two guns and some ammo and I've already been to target practice at the range."[7] Specific details are an indicator that substantial thought, planning, and preparation have already been taken. This suggests a higher risk of the person following through on the threat. Details that are specific but not logical or plausible—such as use of hundreds of pounds of plutonium bombs or rocket launchers—may indicate a less serious threat.

Although this can be an important clue to their mental state and temperament," no correlation has been established between the emotional intensity in a threat and the risk that it will be carried out."[8] Some individuals may be more dramatic than others, but this intensity is not correlated with an increased likelihood of carrying out a threat.

Precipitating stressors, sometimes referred to as trigger events, are incidents, circumstances, reactions, or situations that may have no direct relevance to the threat but nonetheless become a catalyst. It is important to note that these events do not cause a violent act, but may push an already unstable person toward acting out.

The impact of precipitating stressors is dependent upon predisposing factors such as underlying personality traits, characteristics, and temperament that predispose an adolescent to fantasize about violence or to act violently. These include a person's vulnerability to loss and depression or their ability to handle stress or disappointment.

Now, it is possible to assess the threat risk level as low, medium, or high. Contact your security team or local law enforcement with assistance in evaluating the threat. Remember to take all threats seriously.

A low-level threat poses minimal risk to the victim and public safety as it is typically vague, indirect, lacks realism, implausible, inconsistent, lacks detail, and the content suggests the person is unlikely to carry it out.[9]

A medium-level threat could possibly be carried out, but it may not appear entirely realistic. It is more direct and concrete with wording that suggests they have given thought as to how the act will be carried out. In addition, there may be a specific statement—such as "I really mean this" or "I'm not joking"—that seeks to convey that it is not an empty threat.[10]

A high-level threat appears to pose imminent and serious danger to others with direct, specific, and plausible details that suggest concrete steps have been taken toward carrying it out.[11] A specific threat might be "On Wednesday morning at 9 am, I will shoot the pastor with my 9 mm semiauto pistol when he is alone in the sanctuary. I'm tired of his self-righteous attitude."

Threat Assessment Approach

The **Four-Pronged Assessment Model** is "designed to assess someone who has made a threat and evaluate the likelihood that threat will actually be carried out."[12] Anyone can deliver a sinister message, but the assessment is based on a "totality of circumstances" to determine if the individual has the **motivation, means, and intent** to carry out a proclaimed threat. The person threatening must be assessed on four dimensions.

1. Personality
2. Family dynamics
3. Religious institution dynamics and the threat-maker's role in them
4. Social dynamics

Personality is "the pattern of collective character, behavioral, temperamental, emotional, and mental traits of an individual" and is a "product of both inherited temperament and environmental influences."[13] Observable behaviors that provide clues to an individual's personality include the following[14]:

1. How they cope with conflicts, disappointments, failures, insults, or other stresses encountered in everyday life.
2. How they express anger or rage, frustration, disappointment, humiliation, sadness, or similar feelings.
3. Do they demonstrate or fail to demonstrate resiliency after a setback, a failure, real or perceived criticism, disappointment, or other negative experiences.
4. Self-esteem and self-perception—how the individual feels about himself, what kind of person he imagines himself to be, and how he believes he appears to others.
5. How they respond to rules, instruction, or authority figures.
6. Do they demonstrate or express a desire or need for control, attention, respect, admiration, confrontation, or other needs.
7. Do they demonstrate or fail to demonstrate empathy with the feelings and experiences of others.
8. Do they internalize or externalize blame. Those that externalize blame hold others responsible for everything negative that happens to them.
9. Do they show that they view others as inferior or with disrespect and condescension?

Family dynamics concerns the behavior, thinking, beliefs, traditions, roles, customs, and values of a threat-maker's family. How are they treated? Are they valued and respected?

Institution dynamics concerns the behavior, thinking, beliefs, traditions, roles, customs, and values of the religious institution. How is the threat-maker viewed by other members of the religious institution? Do they have any authority within the religious institution? Do they participate when volunteers are called for?

Social dynamics concerns the behavior, thinking, beliefs, traditions, roles, customs, and values of the community the threat-maker is a part of. Are they a leader within their community? What role do they play?

Threat Assessment—Cautions

The following cautions should be considered when making a determination of the seriousness of a threat:[15]

1. There is no magic formula to indicate who will actually carry out a threat.
2. Look for patterns of behavior as "no one or two traits or characteristics should be considered in isolation or given more weight than the others."[16]
3. Behavior is an expression of personality, but one day may not reflect an individual's real personality or typical behavior pattern. Anyone can have a bad day. It is the consistency of behavior that should be noted.
4. A threat assessment is NOT a substitute for clinical diagnosis of mental illness even though many of the behaviors and traits listed are seen in depressed individuals with narcissistic personality characteristics and other possible mental health problems.[17]

Recognizing threats can be very difficult for a number of reasons.[18]

1. Commonality of violent language: Common phrases used by youth and adults alike often refer to violence. We often use these phrases when frustrated, but we don't actually mean them. This common language makes it more difficult for people to know when someone is serious.
   a. Our football team killed them last night!
   b. I'm so mad I could punch her.
   c. Just shoot me!
2. Outrageous claims: Some people make outrageous claims in an attempt to get attention or to make others think they are cool or someone to be feared.
3. Empty threats: In several school shooting cases, perpetrators had threatened violence so many times without acting upon it that other students simply did not believe them. However, this leads to the problem of escalating commitment in which they feel pressured to commit a violent act or risk losing further esteem in the eyes of their peers.
4. Fear of labeling: Many people don't want to be a "tattletale" or "snitch" as this can cause problems with their peers. Others may fear labeling someone as potentially violent when they are not.

Now that we've explained how to conduct a threat assessment, it is time to look at some potential threats.

Signs of a Person Being Under the Influence of Chemical Substances[19]

1. Alcohol
   a. Slurred speech
   b. Inability to coordinate movements
   c. Euphoria
   d. Dizziness
2. Narcotics
   a. Drowsiness
   b. Inability to concentrate
   c. Apathy
   d. Slowed physical activity
   e. Constriction of the pupils
   f. Flushing of the face and neck
   g. Constipation
   h. Nausea
   i. Vomiting
   j. Slowed breathing
3. Stimulants
   a. Agitation
   b. Hostility
   c. Panic
   d. Aggression
   e. Suicidal or homicidal tendencies
   f. Paranoia, sometimes accompanied by both auditory and visual hallucinations
   g. Dizziness
   h. Tremors
   i. Headache

    j. Flushed skin

    k. Chest pain with palpitations

    l. Excessive sweating

    m. Vomiting

    n. Abdominal cramps

4. Depressants

    a. Slurred speech

    b. Loss of motor coordination

    c. Weakness

    d. Headache

    e. Light-headedness

    f. Blurred vision

    g. Dizziness

    h. Nausea

    i. Vomiting

    j. Low blood pressure

    k. Slowed breathing

5. Hallucinogens

    a. Hallucinations

    b. Muscle tension

    c. Tremors

    d. Involuntary teeth clenching

    e. Muscle cramps

    f. Nausea

    g. Faintness

    h. Chills

    i. Sweating

    j. Blurred vision

    k. Deaths generally occur due to suicide, accidents, and dangerous behavior, or due to the person inadvertently eating poisonous plants.

6. Anabolic steroids

    a. Can cause dramatic mood swings

    b. Increased feelings of hostility

    c. Impaired judgment

    d. Increased levels of aggression

    e. When users stop taking steroids, they may experience depression.

    f. That may be severe enough to lead them to commit suicide.

    g. Anabolic steroid use may also cause psychological dependency.

7. Inhalants

    a. Can cause damage to the parts of the brain that control thinking, moving, seeing, and hearing

    b. Cognitive abnormalities can range from mild impairment to severe dementia

    c. Slows down the body's function

    d. Slurred speech

    e. Inability to coordinate movements

    f. Euphoria

    g. Dizziness

    h. After heavy use, they may feel drowsy for several hours and experience a lingering headache

    i. Symptoms of long-term inhalant abusers include weight loss, muscle weakness, disorientation, inattentiveness, lack of coordination, irritability, depression, and damage to the nervous system and other organs

    j. Paint or stains on body or clothing

    k. Spots or sores around the mouth

    l. Red or runny eyes or nose

    m. Chemical breath odor

    n. Drunk, dazed, or dizzy appearance

    o. Nausea

    p. Loss of appetite

    q. Anxiety

    r. Excitability

    s. Irritability

Detailed information about commonly abused substances can be found on the Drug Enforcement Administration's Website at http://www.justice.gov/dea/docs/drugs_of_abuse_2011.pdf.

Cautions

Some legally prescribed medications can also have adverse effects on the verbal, physical, and mental behavior of an individual. Possible side effects are numerous but may include bloodshot eyes, blurred vision, loss of equilibrium, hallucinations, excessive sweating, heart palpitations, loss of coordination, and inability to focus or concentrate.

It is also possible that someone could have a physical ailment that affects their behavior in a manner that makes appear to be under the influence of drugs. Victims of a mild stroke may slur their words and have difficulty maintaining their balance. Diabetics whose sugar is too low may also have coordination issues as well as difficulty answering simple questions. In both of these cases, simply talking calmly to the individual and contacting emergency medical services will handle the situation effectively.

What to Do

Someone who is under chemical influence may not respond the way a normal individual would. Remain calm and find out what they want. Try to move them to an area where they will not disrupt activities. If they are violent or belligerent, contact your security team or local law enforcement.

Mental Illness

These are some brief facts regarding mental illness in the United States as collected by the National Alliance on Mental Illness.[19]

- One in four adults—61.5 million—experiences mental illness in a given year.
- One in 17 adults—13.6 million—lives with a serious mental illness such as schizophrenia, major depression, or bipolar disorder.

- 1.1% or 2.4 million adults live with schizophrenia.
- 2.6% or 6.1 million adults live with bipolar disorder.
- 6.7% or 14.8 million adults live with major depression.
- 18.1% or 42 million adults live with anxiety disorders such as panic disorder, obsessive-compulsive disorder, posttraumatic stress disorder, generalized anxiety, and phobias.
- 9.2 million adults have co-occurring mental health and addiction disorders.
- 26% of homeless adults staying in shelters live with serious mental illness.
- 46% of homeless adults live with severe mental illness and/or substance use disorders.
- 60% of adults with a mental illness received no mental health services in the previous year.

The National Alliance on Mental Illness defines mental illness as "a medical condition that disrupts a person's thinking, feeling, mood, ability to relate to others, and daily functioning," and mental illnesses "often result in a diminished capacity for coping with the ordinary demands of life."[20] As the preceding facts show, large numbers of Americans are affected by a multitude of mental disorders including anxiety disorders; Autism Spectrum disorders; Attention-Deficit/Hyperactivity Disorder (ADD/ADHD); Bipolar Disorder; Borderline Personality Disorder; depression; dissociative disorders; dual diagnosis: substance abuse and mental illness; eating disorders; Obsessive-Compulsive Disorder (OCD); Panic Disorder; Posttraumatic Stress Disorder; Schizoaffective Disorder; Schizophrenia; Seasonal Affective Disorder; and Tourette's Syndrome.

As each has its own symptoms and characteristics, it is not possible to list all of the possible signs. In addition, not everyone with a mental illness will show all of these signs or even any of them. These are just some of the more obvious indicators. Often, it takes time to notice changes in behavior that indicate a mental health issue. In addition, observing these characteristics cannot take the place of a clinical diagnosis.

What to Do

For individuals showing signs of mental illness, the best thing to do is keep them calm and get them professional help and counseling. Most are not violent, but avoid touching them or making them feel as though they have no avenue of escape. Refer them to mental health services. Remain calm and nonjudgmental, and speak in a soft, clear tone. Resources for helping those with mental illness can be found on the National Alliance on Mental Illness's Website designed specifically for religious institutions called NAMI FaithNet at http://www.nami.org/Template.cfm?section=Find_Support. Other resources are listed there as well.

Steps for Outreach for Those with Mental Illness[21]

1. Get approval from senior leaders.
2. Establish a task force comprised of those with a mental illness, family members, health professionals, and a few members who are leaders with no previous involvement with mental illness.

3. Educate yourselves and your group on types of mental illness, treatments, and resources
4. Provide a support group for family members.
5. Provide ministry with those who have a mental illness.

Suspicious Behaviors Indicating Criminal Activity

1. Individual appears to be nervous and looking around
2. Inappropriate clothing, particularly for the weather, such as baggy clothes or big coats
3. Carrying bags or large purses
4. Not focusing on the service and does not participate in activities
5. Leaves the service to wander through the facility
6. Leaves the service after just a brief encounter
7. Not friendly
8. Does not make eye contact and may even be wearing sunglasses indoors
9. Found wandering through the building and has a weak excuse
10. Appears to be angry

Early Warning Signs of Potential Workplace Violence

Workplace violence is a serious concern. Religious organizations need to be aware that disgruntled staff, employees, or even volunteers can potentially become violent.

Baron outlines 14 early warning signs of potential workplace violence.[22]

1. Attendance problems
2. Impact on supervisor/manager's time
3. Decreased productivity
4. Inconsistent work patterns
5. Poor on-the-job relationships
6. Concentration problems
7. Safety issues
8. Poor health and hygiene
9. Unusual or changed behavior
10. Fascination with guns or firearms
11. Signs of revengeful behavior such as sabotage, character assassination, threats, or vandalism[23]
12. Evidence of possible drug or alcohol use or abuse
13. Evidence of serious stress in the employee's personal life
14. Continual blame and excuses
15. Unshakable depression

There is no single indicator that can accurately predict who will act violently toward others.[24] Therefore, you should look for patterns of behavior and signs of escalation. Persons that exhibit behavioral warning signs in more than one category or display behavior that increases in frequency or intensity are more likely to act violently than someone who only displays one warning sign once.

Warning Signs of Potential/Impending Violence

Individuals who are potentially violent often exhibit the following observable characteristics.[25]

1. Facial color becomes whiter or much lighter as oxygen goes to other parts of the body in preparation for physical exertion.
2. Eyebrows and head drop.
3. Breathing becomes very rapid and deep.
4. There are changes in the person's stance.
5. Verbalizations often stop or become strained.
6. The person rocks back and forth, then suddenly stops all movement.
7. They break eye contact and look at targeted areas of the body.
8. Their body drops or slightly dips.

If you witness a cluster of these signals, get away from them and get help.[26] Maintain good defensive body language such as standing with one leg slightly ahead of the other, maintaining eye contact, keeping head and shoulders straight, and keeping your hands in front.[27]

Domestic Violence

Violence can touch your facility in the form of domestic violence. It is important to recognize the signs of possible victimization and get the individual help. In many cases, the abuser attacks and even kills the victim at their place of work or another place, such as a religious institution, the victim frequents. Abusers often attack others nearby in their efforts to kill their primary target.

Signs of Domestic Violence Victimization

The American Bar Association's Commission on Domestic Violence as well as the FBI's Workplace Violence booklet suggests the following observable behavior as evidence of possible domestic violence victimization[28]:

1. Tardiness or unexplained absences
2. Frequent and often unplanned use of leave time
3. Anxiety
4. Lack of concentration
5. Change in job performance
6. Tendency to remain isolated from others or reluctance to participate in social events
7. Discomfort when communicating with others
8. Disruptive phone calls or email
9. Sudden or unexplained requests to be moved from public workplace areas
10. Frequent financial problems indicating a lack of access to money
11. Unexplained bruises or injuries
12. Noticeable change in makeup to cover injuries

13. Inappropriate clothes that can hide bruises such as long sleeves or turtlenecks worn in summer or sunglasses worn indoors
14. Disruptive visits from current or former intimate partner
15. Sudden changes of address
16. Reluctance to divulge where they are staying
17. Acting uncharacteristically moody, depressed, or distracted
18. Being the victim of vandalism or threats

What to Do

The most dangerous time for a victim of domestic violence is often when a restraining order has been issued or divorce is finalized. The former partner may retaliate violently by attacking those they perceive as having helped their victim break free. This includes anyone who counseled them, provided aid or support, or simply listened to them. Anyone who is in the way of them reaching their intended target can also become a victim. However, there are a few things you can do to help victims of domestic violence.

1. Be responsive if someone asks for help.
2. Maintain their confidentiality.
3. Work with the victim, law enforcement, security, and other community resources to develop a workplace safety plan for the victim.[29]
4. Adjust their work schedule or grant leave if the victim requests it. Maintain communication with them during their absence.[30]
5. Have information about domestic violence available, including services available to both victims and perpetrators.
6. Honor all civil protection orders.
7. Advise and assist supervisors and managers with corrective or disciplinary action against perpetrators.[31]

It is important to try to help the perpetrators of domestic violence as well as the victims. There are certified treatment programs for perpetrators that they can be referred to for help.[32] However, be prepared for them to refuse help.

Meeting with a Potentially Violent Person

You may meet with a potentially violent person for various reasons. If you know the person is potentially violent, there are several things you can do to increase your security.[33]

1. Ensure a thorough threat assessment has been conducted before you deal with the person.
2. Think through all of the what-ifs and how you will respond.
3. Develop a prepared script and try to keep it.
4. Don't conduct the encounter alone.
5. Prepare your environment.
   a. Remove any items that could be used as a weapon such as heavy blunt objects or sharp ones.
   b. Sit facing the door.
   c. Make sure an exit is clear.

6. Do not wear clothing or jewelry that could be used to choke you.
7. Keep your hair out of the way so it cannot be grabbed.
8. Program speed dial for security or law enforcement.
9. Make sure you have established a signal system to notify others that you need help.
10. Mentally prepare yourself for anger, blame, insults, and verbal abuse. Plan appropriate responses.
11. Treat them with respect and sensitivity.
12. Prepare for the worst and trust your instincts.

Confrontation Management and De-Escalation Techniques

When dealing with any of the preceding, it is important to use confrontation management, conflict resolution, and de-escalation techniques to prevent a situation from getting worse.

1. Keep enough distance at first.
2. Allow them to cool off, but don't tell them to "calm down."
3. Approach slowly and calmly.
4. Do not grab or even touch the person.[34]
5. Try to guide them to an area away from others, but do not let yourself be trapped.
6. Listen to them without interruption.
7. Treat them with respect and sensitivity.
8. Use reassuring gestures.
9. Speak in a calm and non-confrontational tone.
10. Remain neutral and nonjudgmental.
11. Show empathy.

Empathy is the most powerful concept in the English language as it absorbs tension.[35] Many people in crisis just want to be listened to and understood.

In their book *Verbal Judo*, the authors list 11 things to never say to someone.[36]

1. Come here!
2. You would not understand.
3. Because those are the rules.
4. It's none of your business.
5. What do you want me to do about it?
6. Calm down!
7. What's your problem?
8. You never… or You always…
9. I'm not going to say this again.
10. I'm doing this for your own good.
11. Why don't you be reasonable?

The preceding phrases come across as judgmental and will likely escalate a tense situation. Instead, focus on the five universal truths to human interactions.[37]

1. People feel the need to be respected.
2. People would rather be asked than be told.

3. People have a desire to know why.
4. People prefer to have options over threats.
5. People want to have a second chance.

Regardless of their mental state, motivation, or actions, most people will respond positively to someone who shows them empathy and respect.

Universal Truths of Human Interaction

1. People feel the need to be respected.
2. People would rather be asked than be told.
3. People have a desire to know why.
4. People prefer to have options over threats.
5. People want to have a second chance.

Final Thoughts

There are many ways in which religious institutions can become vulnerable to potential violence. However, with sound policies and procedures and proper training, the risks can be reduced. As always, remain alert to potential danger and aware of your surroundings. If you are the least bit uncomfortable with someone, do not meet with them alone. Do not hesitate to contact security or law enforcement if their behavior becomes threatening. Getting at-risk individuals the professional assistance they need is the best thing you can do to help them.

End Notes

1. Kerr K. M., *Workplace Violence* (Massachusetts: Butterworth-Heinemann, 2010).
2. Critical Incident Response Group and National Center for the Analysis of Violence Crime, *The School Shooter: A Threat Assessment Perspective* (1999). Retrieved from www.fbi.gov/stats-services/publications/school-shooter.
3. Ibid, p. 6.
4. See note 2 above.
5. See note 2 above, p. 7.
6. See note 2 above.
7. See note 2 above.
8. See note 2 above, p. 8.
9. See note 2 above.
10. See note 2 above.
11. See note 2 above.
12. See note 2 above, p. 10.
13. See note 2 above, p. 11.
14. See note 2 above.
15. See note 2 above, p. 15.

16. http://www.justice.gov/dea/docs/drugs_of_abuse_2011.pdf.

17. See note 2 above.

18. Christensen L. W., *Surviving a School Shooting: A Plan of Action for Parents, Teachers, and Students* (Boulder: Paladin Press, 2008).

19. http://www.nami.org/factsheets/mentalillness_factsheet.pdf.

20. http://www.nami.org/Template.cfm?Section=By_Illness.

21. www.nami.org/MSTemplate.cfm?Section=Ministry_With_Those_With_a_Mental_Illness&Template=/ContentManagement/ContentDisplay.cfm&ContentID=32331&MicrositeID=176.

22. Baron A., *Violence in the Workplace* (San Francisco: Pathfinder Publishing, 2001).

23. See note 1 above.

24. Philpott D. and Grimme D., *The Workplace Violence Prevention Handbook* (Maryland: Government Institutes, 2009).

25. See note 1 above.

26. See note 1 above.

27. See note 1 above.

28. See note 24 above.

29. See note 24 above.

30. See note 24 above.

31. See note 24 above.

32. See note 24 above.

33. See note 24 above.

34. Johnson K., *Classroom Crisis: The Teacher's Guide* (Alameda: Hunter House Publishing, 2004).

35. Thompson G. J. and Jenkins J. B., *Verbal Judo: The Gentle Art of Persuasion* (New York: William Morrow, 2013).

36. Ibid.

37. Ibid.

Reacting to an Event in Progress ⁹

Violent actions or assaults in religious institutions are not just an active shooter situation, although that is what makes headlines and endless news reports. They involve all types of criminal activity including property damage. They include, but are not limited to, verbal harm, physical harm, sexual harassment, threats, bullying, and bringing weapons on the property. Violent actions or assaults affect not only those immediately involved but also the leaders, staff, and attendees of the religious institution as well as the surrounding community.

Despite all of your careful planning, a crisis event is now occurring. How do you handle it? In large part, your actions are dictated by the type of crisis. They should also be guided by your established plans, policies, and procedures. If your staff has been trained according to established plans, they should be able to quickly assume their roles, perform their designated tasks, and control the situation with relative efficiency.

Effective response is dependent upon quick thinking and quick actions. There is no time to hesitate; so once you have decided on a course of action, you must commit to it.

Your first task should always be to get a response force to the incident, whether it is your security team, private security, or law enforcement. Even with a security team or private security response force, it is essential that you also contact local law enforcement. However, if multiple areas are affected, it may delay law enforcement's ability to get to your facility quickly. Fire and emergency medical services will also be contacted simultaneously with law enforcement by calling 911.

Declaring a Crisis

Reacting to an event in progress involves several steps[1]:

1. Potential crisis recognition
2. Notify the teams
3. Assess the situation
4. Declare a crisis
5. Execute the plan

First, you recognize that a potential crisis is occurring. This involves identifying and recognizing danger signals.[2] Leaders have a responsibility to recognize and report potential crimes.

The second step is to notify security teams, the threat assessment committee, and other individuals who may be immediately affected by the event. Notifications should be timely, clear, and through a variety of procedures and technologies.[3]

The next step is to assess the situation along two parameters. Problem assessment is the decision-making process that will determine the nature of the event to be addressed.[4] A severity assessment determines the seriousness of the event and any associated long-term costs.[5] Other factors to consider are the size of the issue, the escalation potential, and the possible impact.[6]

The point at which a crisis is declared should be clearly defined in the emergency response plan, be documented, and fit very specific parameters.[7] Who has the responsibility for declaring a crisis as well as first and second alternates should also be identified. Declaring a crisis can trigger activities such as evacuation, shelter, team deployment, emergency activation, and operational changes.[8] Other activities as defined in the response plan may be initiated as well.

Execution of the plan involves saving lives, reducing chances of further injuries or death, protecting assets, restoring critical business processes, safeguarding your reputation, and controlling media coverage.

Communication and Notification

When an incident is in progress, it is extremely important to communicate with others that something is happening. This is important for summoning assistance as well as preventing others from becoming potential victims.

Notification policies and procedures should be in place including who notifies whom, how, and when. Do not assume others are aware of what is going on. Lack of communication could result in more casualties. You want to ensure that everyone is aware of what is happening, so they can protect themselves as well.

How Do You Notify Others?

In the event of an incident, there should be a facility-wide notification system so others can be alerted to the presence of danger. Email is not effective unless everyone has smart phones. Virginia Tech was criticized for their use of email when most students and staff were not able to access it in a timely manner. However, texts or other instant notification methods are necessary. It is not advisable to use a public address system or music system, if there is one, as that will likely cause a panic as well as alert the assailant.

You should not use the fire alarm. In Jonesboro, Arkansas, one of the two shooters pulled the fire alarm then went into the woods where his partner was set up in a sniper's position.[9] The first students and teachers outside the doors were the ones shot. It also confuses people as to what the real danger is. Some people ignore the fire alarm thinking it is simply a drill, further reducing the fire alarm as an effective warning system for other incidents.

Code systems should be used to notify others of impending danger. The system should be documented in the emergency plans and included in training for all staff and volunteers.

There are several types of codes to choose from as outline by Christensen (2008).[10] The most important thing is to be consistent in using them and to make sure that everyone knows what they mean. Do not make the notification system too complex or it will be ineffective.

1. **Color Code**: The PA system can be used to alert faculty and staff by saying "Code Orange" or whatever color is the designated alert.[11] It does not matter which color used, so long as everyone is aware of what it means.
2. **Code Word**: Instead of a color code, a word can be chosen to signify an armed intruder is in the building, such as "Code Adam." It should be easily remembered and recognized.
3. **Bell Alarm**: A building-wide audible alarm distinct from a fire alarm is used. The alarm may signify that individuals are to shelter-in-place or evacuate.[12] This can be expensive and costly, but may be highly effective if there are only a few different alarm sounds to recognize.
4. **Phone Tree**: Employ an interoffice phone tree to warn that a dangerous situation exists.
5. **Personal Alarm System**: Leaders and staff can carry with them a personal aerosol alarm or other device that emits a loud shriek, but should be activated only in the event of great danger.

Who Do You Notify?

Once you are able to do so without compromising safety, use the established communication system to notify everyone present in the facility of the incident and any potential threats. Inform them of their next course of action and any other necessary actions that are important to maintain their safety. Notify them of any potential threats.

Individuals to notify include but are not limited to the following:

- Members and attendees
- Staff and volunteers
- Visitors
- Notify anyone else you may encounter to exit the building immediately.

Where Do You Notify People?

During the course of the day, individuals may be in various locations throughout the building. If they are outside but still on facility grounds, you do not want them to enter the building. They may be able to summon help more quickly if they are out of the immediate danger zone. As soon as feasible, you want to notify those who are at offsite locations so they do not return to the facility until the danger has passed.

Notify Emergency Services

Emergency situations should be reported to law enforcement by dialing 911. Be prepared to provide the 911 operator with as much information as possible, such as the following:

- What is happening
- Where you are located, including building name and room number if applicable
- Number of people at your specific location

- Number of people at facility. This is likely to be an estimate but make an educated guess.
- Injuries, if any, including the number of injured and types of injuries
- Your name and other information as requested
- Try to provide information in a calm, clear manner so that the 911 operator can quickly relay your information to responding law enforcement and emergency personnel.
- Number of assailants
- Gender, race, and age of the assailant
- Language or commands used by the assailant
- Clothing color and style
- Physical features, e.g., height, weight, facial hair, glasses
- Type of weapons, e.g., handgun, rifle, shotgun, explosives
- Description of any backpack or bag
- Do you recognize the assailant? Do you know their name?
- What exactly did you hear, e.g., explosions, gunshots, etc.

Bomb Threats

Bomb threats are often hoaxes, but you cannot afford to take a chance. Take all threats seriously. Gather as much information as you can and report to the police and/or your security team.

If the threat is called in, you should document the following as the call is happening:

1. How does the caller sound? Angry? Calm? Excited?
2. Is the voice familiar?
3. What kind of background sounds can you hear?
4. What type of language did they use?[13] Well-educated? Incoherent?
5. What are their exact words?
6. Record anything else you can notice.
7. Note the date and time of call.
8. Who did they call? Did they ask for a specific person?
9. Did they call a cell phone, a main number, or an office number?
10. Where is the bomb?
11. Who is the target?
12. Why was it set?
13. What are the caller's demands?
14. What type of bomb?

If the threat is written, the following should be documented:

1. Who found it?
2. Was anyone else present?
3. Where was it found and/or how was it delivered?
4. When was it found or delivered?
5. Did anyone touch it?
6. Have any previous threats been received?
7. What are their demands?
8. Are there any distinguishing characteristics of the paper or writing?

Regardless of how the threat is received, you must remain calm, and do not panic others. You will need to report it to law enforcement. They will decide on a plan of action including whether or not to evacuate the building. Individuals should gather in a safe spot to account for everyone. The gathering point should be far enough away that no one will be injured in case a bomb is detonated.

Other Threats

Not all threats received are bomb threats. Threats can be made against the facility for other reasons. These threats can be received via mail, email, phone call, or hand delivered. Protocol for handling these threats is similar to that of bomb threats.

1. Take threats seriously.
2. Do not respond to them.
3. Do not hang up if the threat is made over the telephone.
4. Call law enforcement.
5. Document the circumstances surrounding receiving the threat including details about wording, demands, and any other distinguishing characteristics.
6. Follow police instructions.

Suspicious Mail or Packages

The following is a list of signs to watch out for[14]:

- Unfamiliar address and sender
- No return address
- Improper or incorrect title, address, or spelling of addressee
- Title without name
- Wrong title with name
- Handwritten or poorly typed address
- Misspellings of common words
- Return address and postmark are not from same area
- Stamps instead of metered mail
- Excessive postage or unusual stamps
- Special handling instructions such as "special delivery open by addressee only"
- Restrictive markings such as "confidential" or "personal"
- Overwrapping or excessive securing material
- Oddly shaped or unevenly weighted packages
- Lumpy or rigid envelopes that are stiffer or heavier than normal
- Lopsided or uneven envelopes
- Oily stains or discolorations
- Strange odors
- Protruding wires or tinfoil
- Visual distractions such as drawings, unusual statements, or hand-drawn postage

This list is not comprehensive. In addition, you should be cautioned that mail or packages exhibiting one or more of these characteristics is not necessarily a threat either. Individuals still use stamps and handwrite addresses.

The most important actions are as follows:

1. Do not to touch the package.
2. Evacuate the area.
3. Contact local law enforcement immediately.

Suspicious Items

Look closely around the area when you arrive at the facility. If you notice anything suspicious, stay away from it, and contact the police. Pay particular attention to large packages or items such as backpacks or coolers that seem to have been left behind or thrown out.

Do not use radios or cell phones anywhere near it as they could trigger a detonation. Do not panic others, but keep them away from the suspicious item as well.

Potential Attacker

Although active-shooter incidents garner the most attention, nonfatal incidents make up the vast majority of incidents of workplace violence.[15] Do not focus solely on guns, as other objects that may be grabbed in the heat of the moment or concealed for a planned attack can be just as deadly.[16] For example, knives, scissors, and other edged weapons are easily concealed until the perpetrator is within striking distance of the victim.

It is important to recognize the potential of objects for use as weapons not only to protect yourself, but to use as a means of incapacitating an attacker if necessary. Any object can be used as a bludgeon including staplers, binders, and other standard office supplies.[17] Chemicals, including many cleaning products, are easily accessible on many work sites. Aerosol sprays can be ignited by a lighter or chemicals can be sprayed or splashed in someone's face, causing chemical burns.

In most cases, it will require time for help to respond. In those instances, you should know what to do to keep yourself, your staff/employees, and your attendees safe. You have several choices when faced with a potential attacker.

1. Escape
2. Hide
3. Intervene verbally
4. Intervene physically

There are several questions you need to answer before deciding upon a course of action.[18]

• Are there others nearby who are willing to assist you in controlling the subject?
• Have you or anyone else notified the others, security, or the police?

- Would it be better for you to flee?
- Is there an avenue of escape available to you?

Escape/Evacuation

Priority number one is safety. Just being a spectator to a fight or verbal altercation can suddenly lead to involvement. By creating distance between the incident and others, you will mitigate the likelihood that something happens to them.

Evacuation or escape is one of the best ways to mitigate damages and prevent loss of life. The best way to avoid being a target is to not be there. Simply run as fast as you can in the opposite direction. Moving targets are harder to hit. Clustering together makes it easier for an adversary to increase the number of casualties. Tell individuals to scatter and run hard away from the assailant.

In order to escape successfully, you need both an opportunity and an avenue of escape.[19] An opportunity is when the adversary is at the opposite end of the room or hall. An avenue of escape is the path closest to a door that is unobstructed. Look for unconventional exits as well. Several students survived the VA Tech shooting by jumping out of windows.

There are several special groups that plans must take into account: special needs and disabled persons, the elderly, and children. These groups will require special assistance and monitoring.

Hide

If escape is not possible, your next option is to conceal yourself and/or others.

1. Close and lock the door.
2. Barricade the door.
3. Turn off the lights.
4. Remain as quiet as possible until police arrive.

Verbal Intervention

In some cases, talking calmly to the adversary may be enough to pacify them. Your goal is to defuse the situation and get the assailant to surrender. The following are techniques to utilize when intervening verbally[20]:

- Maintain a cool demeanor. Do not show anger, nervousness, or fear. Project calmness.
- Do not tell them to "calm down." This only makes people angrier, and it is often perceived as passing judgment.
- Move and speak slowly, quietly, and confidently.
- Maintain a relaxed yet attentive posture.
- Position yourself at a right angle instead of directly in front of the other person. Make sure you are not blocking your access to an exit.
- Focus your attention on the other person to let them know that you are interested in what he or she has to say. Look them in the eye and nod as they speak.
- Ask how you can help.

- Practice active listening.
- Stay neutral no matter what the person says.
- Acknowledge the person's feelings. Indicate that you understand that he or she is upset.
- Ask for small, specific favors, such as asking to move to a quieter area.
- Establish ground rules if unreasonable behavior persists.
- Calmly describe the consequences of any violent behavior.
- Use delaying tactics that will give the person time to calm down. For example, offer them water, a place to sit, or a tissue.
- Direct the individual to an area where they can calm down and where there are not any objects they can throw or kick.[21]

It is important to maintain some physical distance from the individual so as not to appear threatening, to refrain from touching the individual unless absolutely necessary, and to remain at arm's length to prevent an attack.[22]

Managing Anxiety

It is important to recognize the signs of anxiety in an individual including sweating, minimal eye contact, face flushing, lip twitching, minimal or excessive talking, constant movement, shallow breathing, and skin color that is darker than normal.[23]

It is critical to give the anxious person physical space.[24] Keep facial expressions and body language supportive and nonthreatening. As these individuals often just want to vent, ask open-ended questions, redirect anger to the past, and avoid blame.[25] Remain calm and confident in your tone and body language.

Managing Verbal Aggression

Anxiety that is not managed properly can become verbal aggression. These individuals often display the characteristics such as darkening or reddening of the face, prolonged eye contact, protruding and stiff lips, quick deep breathing, stiffened head and shoulders, violent gestures, and belligerent behavior such as yelling and cursing.[26]

At this stage, the person may be testing the situation. Follow the same guidelines as when dealing with anxiety: Provide personal space, allow them to vent, and remain calm and supportive.[27] If they cannot deescalate on their own, communicate clearly reasonable and enforceable limits.

Physical Intervention

This can be difficult for those who believe in nonviolence. However, you must remember that others are in danger. Hurting the attacker will potentially save many more lives. When considering physical intervention, think about how your size, strength, and physical condition compares to theirs.[28]

Someone Threatening with a Weapon[29]

- Quietly signal for help.
- Keep your cool and do not aggravate his/her rage.
- Stall and personalize.
- Negotiate.
- Respect the weapon, but focus on the person holding it.
- Look for opportunities for getting yourself and others to safety.

Breaking up a Fight[30]

- Get assistance; intervening alone is dangerous.
- Remove the audience; onlookers fuel the fire.
- Avoid stepping between combatants; it shifts aggression to you.
- Separate combatants.

Unarmed Attacker

If the assailant appears unarmed, recognize that they may have a concealed weapon. In addition, take note of any environmental weapons within their reach such as trash cans, chairs, staplers, or other heavy objects.[31]

Recommendations for confronting the individual include the following as outlined by Christensen (2008):[32]

- You and anyone else who is around should grab any object within reach—stapler, coffee cup, paperweight, trash can, etc.—and throw it at him or her. Be aggressive and keep throwing things until you have the opportunity to move in. You may have to advance first as others are hesitant to initiate physical contact.
- When he bends to cover himself, rush him, take him to the floor, and dog-pile him. Rush him with a chair, desk, table, or other object of comparable size, and use it to force him to the floor or against a wall and then dog-pile him.
- To confuse him, you and three others rush from his left, right, front, and rear.
- Understand that it is likely you will be punched, clawed, kicked, and bitten as you struggle to subdue him.

Attacker with Improvised Weapon

If the attacker has an improvised weapon, i.e., something they just grabbed such as a chair or heavy object, you should consider the following questions before acting.[33]

- Is there an avenue of escape available to you?
- What environmental weapon is within your reach?
- How effective does he/she seem with the object in his hands?
    - Is the object large and cumbersome?
    - Alternatively, is it easily wielded and sharp?
- When he swings the object, does he maintain his balance or does he stumble or fall?
- Is he/she right-handed or left-handed?
- Are you facing him alone or with others willing to deal with him physically?

The confrontation techniques are the same as for an unarmed attacker.[34] If the attacker flees, let him go, then close and lock the door behind him.[35]

Final Thoughts

It takes cooperation and communication to identify threats and respond appropriately. All staff should be trained. They should rehearse and practice frequently so their actions become second nature.

It is important that the administration support and enforce recommendations made by staff and attendees concerning at-risk individuals.

- Reporting does little good if the reports are not followed up on.
- Just because you do not think there is a problem that does not mean there is not one.
- Just because it has not happened yet does not mean it will never happen.
- It is important to remain vigilant, to plan, and to rehearse, so when the unthinkable happens, you can react quickly and decisively to save lives.
- You *can* make a difference.

Situations evolve rapidly, and there is no textbook case; so, do not worry that you are doing the wrong thing. All anyone can expect of you is that you do what you have been trained to do.

End Notes

1. ASIS Commission on Standards and Guidelines, *Business Continuity Guideline: A Practical Approach for Emergency Preparedness, Crisis Management, and Disaster Recovery* (Alexandria: ASIS, International, 2005).
2. Ibid.
3. Ibid.
4. Ibid.
5. Ibid.
6. Ibid.
7. Ibid.
8. Ibid.
9. Langman, P., *Why Kids Kill: Inside the Minds of School Shooters* (New Yok: Palgrave MacMillan, 2009).
10. Christensen L. W., *Surviving a School Shooting: A Plan of Action for Parents, Teachers, and Students* (Boulder: Paladin Press, 2008).
11. Ibid.
12. Ibid.
13. Tyska L. A. and Fennelly L. J., *Physical Security: 150 Things You Should Know* (Massachusetts: Butterworth-Heinemann, 2000).
14. Ibid.
15. Critical Incident Response Group, *Workplace Violence: Issues in Response* (U.S. Department of Justice, 2002).
16. See note 9 above.
17. Lanier S. L., *Workplace Violence Before, During, and After* (Alexandria: ASIS International, 2003).
18. See note 10 above.
19. Ibid.

20. Kerr K. M., *Workplace Violence* (Massachusetts: Butterworth-Heinemann, 2010).

21. See note 17 above.

22. Philpott D. and Grimme D., *The Workplace Violence Prevention Handbook* (Maryland: Government Institutes, 2009).

23. See note 20 above.

24. See note 20 above.

25. See note 20 above.

26. See note 20 above.

27. See note 20 above.

28. See note 10 above.

29. See note 22 above.

30. Ibid.

31. See note 10 above.

32. Ibid.

33. Ibid.

34. Ibid.

35. Ibid.

Responding to an Active Shooter

10

In June 2013, FEMA issued a report entitled "Guide for Developing High-Quality Emergency Operations Plans for Houses of Worship." The document can be accessed on the FEMA Website at http://www.fema.gov/media-library/assets/documents/33007. Issuance of the report indicates that FEMA thinks active shooter events in houses of worship are a legitimate concern.

Some basic facts about active shooting incidents emphasize the need for religious institutions to prepare for and respond to active shooter incidents.

- The average active-shooter incident lasts 12 min. Thirty-seven percent last less than 5 min.[1]
- Average initial police response time is 12 min.[2]
- James Holmes killed 12 and wounded 58 in less than 15 min.[3]
- Seung-Hui Cho killed 32 people and wounded 17 in less than 11 min in 2007.[4] He killed himself as well.
- Overwhelmingly, the offender is a single shooter (98%) who kills himself/herself in 40% of cases.[5]
- In 10% of the cases, the shooter stops and walks away. In 20% of the cases, the shooter goes mobile, moving to another location.[6]
- Forty-three percent of the time, the crime is over before police arrive. In 57% of the shootings, an officer arrives while the shooting is still underway.[7]
- The shooter often stops as soon as he/she hears or sees law enforcement, sometimes turning his anger or aggression on law enforcement.[8]

In Chapter 9, we discussed responding to incidents including assaults with or without blunt or edged weapons. This chapter will focus on active shooter events.

An active shooter event can be one of several types of situations:

1. Workplace violence by former or current staff or volunteers
2. Domestic violence
3. Hate crime
4. Random act

Despite the difference in motivation, the response is similar in each of these situations. Effective response is dependent upon quick thinking and quick reactions. You will have little time to weigh your options and make a decision. During high-stress situations, your instincts take over. Sound policies and procedures, comprehensive training, and effective practice will ensure that you can respond quickly and effectively to any situation that may arise. This section provides tips on how to respond. However, you will have to make the final choice yourself during an incident.

Active shooter events are unpredictable and evolve rapidly. These situations require you to think and to decide quickly on a course of action. Reacting quickly and decisively can stop an incident and save lives.

Factors that Affect Decision-Making

The nature of the situation makes it difficult to make decisions. There are several reasons for this.[9]

1. Lack of warning
2. Rapidly evolving situation
3. Chaos, confusion, disbelief, and fear
4. Physiological changes
5. Lack of information
6. Previous rehearsal

During a shooting, you will have little advance notice; your warning may be recognizing the sound of gunfire, hearing screams, or seeing individuals fall down bleeding. You may become paralyzed with fear and unable to comprehend what is happening. This can slow your decision-making and reaction time.

Rapidly evolving situation: You will not have time to methodically evaluate different courses of action. You will have to react quickly.

Chaos, confusion, disbelief, and fear: When a situation occurs, it will be chaotic as people scramble to grasp what is happening. There will be a great deal of confusion and fear as well as disbelief that it is actually happening.

Physiological changes: The body's fight or flight response kicks in during highly stressful situations causing accelerated heart rate, shallow breathing, and an adrenaline surge.[10]

Lack of information: You will not have all of the facts, so it may be difficult to judge the situation accurately and respond accordingly.

If you and your staff/attendees have planned, studied, and rehearsed scenarios and responses, you will react instinctively. This will shorten your reaction time.

Preparation

Preparing for an active shooter event should begin weeks or months before an incident occurs. Think strategically about your environment so you can react quickly during a situation.

1. Examine objects as potential weapons. When you look at an object, think to yourself "it would really hurt if that was smashed on someone's head, hand, etc."[11]
2. Examine environment for potential barricades. Heavy furniture works best.
3. Examine environment for hiding places for perpetrators and potential victims.
4. Examine environment for escape routes for employees, attendees, yourself, and the assailant.
5. If you are in a room with a door, stay there, and secure the door with locks and barricades.[12]
6. If you are in a hallway, get into a room, and secure the door with locks and barricades.[13]
7. As a last resort, attempt to take the active shooter down. When the shooter is at close range and you cannot flee, your chance of survival is much greater if you try to incapacitate him/her.[14]

FEMA's active shooter training follows three simple courses of action: run, hide, and fight.[15] This online training is free and should be taken by staff members. It can be accessed at http://training.fema.gov/EMIWeb/IS/courseOverview.aspx?code=is-907.

Immediate Response to Severe Incident[16]

1. Remove or warn other potential victims.
2. Move to a safe area.
3. Call for immediate assistance.
4. Remove or secure potential weapons.
5. Secure the environment.
6. Attend to first aid needs.

Run

At the first available safe opportunity, move away from the suspect. Do not allow others to become stagnant targets. Individuals need to scatter in different directions so long as they are not in the path of the shooter. If they cannot run zigzag, just tell them to run hard.

Help others escape if possible, but evacuate even if others do not agree to go with you.[17] If they are evacuating with you, aid each other in escape by having one group watching while another group moves to cover further down the desired path. This not only potentially maintains eyes on the threat, but it also provides security.

Do not attempt to move the wounded as it the responsibility of emergency response services.

Leave your belongings. Your life is more important than any object. Stopping or going back to retrieve something can delay you long enough to become a victim. Tell individuals to simply run. They can replace their belongings later.

Hide

If escape is not possible, your next best option is to hide. Close and lock all windows and doors. If doors open into the room, barricade them with furniture.

If you want to shelter-in-place, there are several things you can do to maximize your chances of survival. Stay away from windows after closing blinds and curtains. Turn off lights. Have everyone remain silent so they can listen for the suspect's movements. By remaining quiet, the perpetrator will not be alerted to the presence of potential victims. Lying on the floor can keep people out of the line of fire. Silence cell phones and other electronic devices to avoid alerting the attacker to your presence.

Use the principles of cover and concealment as you hide. Cover shields you from bullets and may prevent the attacker from seeing you.[18] Look around your current location for objects that can effectively cover you such as cement walls, heavy cabinets, metal doors, or large equipment. Cover can protect you when the shooter knows you are in the room but cannot see you.[19] They will likely not waste ammunition shooting indiscriminately at objects in hopes of catching people. They will likely move on to where they know there are unprotected people.

Concealment hides you from the attacker's view, but it will not protect you from bullets. Closets, hollow spaces, under desks, or behind equipment are examples of places that may provide cover. It is most effective if the attacker does not know you are there. If the room appears empty, the attacker will probably move on to other targets.[20]

Intervene

Intervention is not just a confrontational assault on active shooters. It is talking them down, providing insight into decision-making, and verbally stopping an altercation. This intervention, no matter how small, can prevent serious harm later on down the road.

When an active shooter incident occurs, you have several options based on the situation. If hiding and locking doors are not feasible, you can draw attention away from others and verbally confront the shooter. More than one incident has been defused by a teacher actually showing interest and talking to an armed student.

You can also physically intervene by either drawing attention away from others or physically acting to neutralize the threat. The option you choose is based on the circumstances including the number of perpetrators, the types of weapons, the layout of the location, and your own abilities.[21]

Fight

In some cases, you may have to physically intervene with the armed suspect. If you must fight back, you need to understand that you may have to put yourself in harm's way to save the lives of others, and that in doing so, you could be seriously injured or killed.

To engage the attacker verbally or physically, you must remain calm and confident. When you are calm, you can think rationally and act more quickly. You can also keep others calm, thereby preventing further injury.

There are several cases in which an individual stopped an active shooter by fighting back.

- A 14-year old in Moses Lake, Washington, armed with two pistols shot four people in class before taking hostages. A teacher rushed him and tackled him to the floor, thereby saving lives.[22]
- After a 14-year old in Edinburg, Pennsylvania, brought a gun to his graduation dance and opened fire killing one student and wounding three others. The banquet hall owner—armed with a shotgun—disarmed, subdued, and held the boy for the police.[23]
- Michael Carneal, a 14-year old in Paducah, Kentucky, killed three and wounded five before he was stopped when another student took him to the ground.[24]

Recognizing Attacker Vulnerabilities

Physical intervention is more effective when timed properly. There are several things to look for that can provide an opportunity for action.

- **Recognize the sound of reloads**: After a 13-year-old boy shot four classmates in Oklahoma, a science teacher approached the boy who was still pulling the trigger on an empty gun; he grabbed the boy's arms and pinned him against a brick wall, saving others' lives.[25]
- **Recognize the sound of an empty gun**: Kip Kinkel was tackled by students after one of his guns ran out of ammunition.[9]

Recognition of these vulnerabilities should be taught in training courses. These instances are when an adversary is most vulnerable and can provide the perfect opportunity for escape or intervention.

What to Do when Law Enforcement Arrives

It will take several minutes for law enforcement and other emergency personnel to arrive on the scene. Their primary purpose is to do the following:

- Stop the shooter.
- Secure the scene.
- Attend to victims.

In order to minimize the chaos when law enforcement arrives, it is important that individuals know how to act. This will prevent those people from becoming inadvertent victims or distracting the police.

When police arrive on scene, they do not know who the perpetrators are, how many there are, or any other pertinent details. Therefore, they have to treat everyone as potential suspects until the threat is neutralized.[26]

- When law enforcement arrives, you must do what you are told.
- Remain calm.
- Move slowly, and keep your hands visible at all times.
- Put down any items in your hands such as bags or jackets.[27]
- Avoid pointing, screaming, or yelling.[28]
- Officers may shout commands and may push individuals to the ground for their safety.[29]
- Avoid making any sudden movements toward officers or attempting to hold on to them.[30]

Final Thoughts

One of the most important characteristics of an active shooter event is that they are planned well in advance. This means that there is a strong probability of preventing the attack. The problem is recognizing the signs. In many cases, the religious institution does not realize they are the target. Therefore, they are not aware of the warning signs until it is too late. However, sound security policies, procedures, and countermeasures will provide some protection.

End Notes

1. Schweit K. W., "Addressing the Problem of the Active Shooter," *FBI Law Enforcement Bulletin* (May 2013). Retrieved from http://www.fbi.gov/stats-services/publications/law-enforcement-bulletin/2013/May/active-shooter.

2. Sinai J., *Active Shooter: A Handbook on Prevention* (Alexandria: ASIS International, 2013).

3. Ibid.

4. Ibid.

5. See note 1 above.

6. See note 1 above.

7. See note 1 above.

8. See note 1 above.

9. Christensen L. W., *Surviving a School Shooting: A Plan of Action for Parents, Teachers, and Students* (Boulder: Paladin Press, 2008).

10. Ibid.

11. Ibid.

12. DHS, *Active Shooter: How to Respond* (October 2008). Retrieved from http://www.dhs.gov/xlibrary/assets/active_shooter_booklet.pdf.

13. Ibid.

14. Ibid.

15. Ibid.

16. Philpott D. and Grimme D., *The Workplace Violence Prevention Handbook* (Maryland: Government Institutes, 2009).

17. See note 2 above.

18. See note 2 above.

19. See note 9 above.

20. See note 9 above.

21. See note 9 above.

22. See note 9 above.

23. See note 9 above.

24. See note 9 above.

25. See note 9 above.

26. See note 9 above.

27. See note 2 above.

28. See note 2 above.

29. See note 12 above.

30. See note 2 above.

Recovering from an Incident

11

Once the initial danger has passed, the incident is far from over. It may take several weeks or even months for a full recovery to occur. Although an event may be over in mere minutes, the effects can last a lifetime.

"Recovery is the process of repairing damage, restoring services and reconstructing facilities after disaster has struck."[1] Recovery is important for the physical, emotional, and psychological well-being of a community that has faced a crisis event.

Incident recovery takes place in three general phases: immediate aftermath, short term, and long term.

Immediate Aftermath

The immediate aftermath of an incident begins with the response phase and ends when the threat has been neutralized. There is likely still shock and confusion. However, it is critical that the extent of the incident be recognized and handled. Organizations have been sued or suffered public relations issues for not taking an event seriously enough.

The immediate aftermath of an incident can include some or all of the following:

1. Making sure everyone is safe
2. Accounting for the whereabouts of everyone in attendance
3. Cooperating with law enforcement, private security, and/or emergency services
4. Performing first aid as needed
5. Notifying loved ones that victims are safe or which hospital they were taken to
6. Reuniting loved ones
7. Handling the media
8. Access control of threatened areas
9. Crowd control
10. Vehicle and pedestrian traffic control
11. Protection against a continuing threat and a search for secondary threats[2]

Once you have reached a safe location or evacuation site, you will likely be held in that area by law enforcement until the situation is under control and all witnesses have been identified and questioned. When the threat has passed, management should engage in post-event assessments and activities including the following:

1. An accounting of all individuals at a designated assembly point is performed to determine if anyone is missing and potentially injured.
2. A method is determined for notifying families of individuals affected by the incident, including notification of any casualties. Notification of casualties may best be handled by law enforcement.
3. The psychological state of individuals at the scene is assessed, and referrals to specialists are made.

As soon as it is safe to do so, provide some sort of first aid for the injured. First aid can be something as simple as stopping the bleeding or elevating a bleeding limb. If untrained, wear gloves and clean any wounds. If certified in first aid through a national organization such as the American Heart Association or American Red Cross, perform needed tasks in which you have been trained. Try to ensure that any injured or immobile individuals are taken somewhere safe or at least somewhere with cover. Make sure to practice universal precautions by wearing gloves and other protective gear and taking care.

Short Term

In the days and weeks that follow, short-term recovery efforts take place. There are a number of considerations that influence the success of recovery efforts. This is heavily dependent upon proper planning as well as actually following established processes when responding to an incident.

Business Continuity

Business continuity is a comprehensive effort to prioritize key business processes, identify significant threats to normal operation, and plan mitigation strategies to ensure effective and efficient organization response to the challenges that surface during and after a crisis.[3]

It occurs in two stages: recovery and resumption. Recovery focuses on getting a business up and running within 30 to 60 days, restoring critical processes, and resuming operations.[4] Resumption is concerned with the long-term process of resuming normal business operations although they may not be restored to the same conditions as prior to the crisis.

Both stages include conducting a business impact analysis (BIA), which is financial analysis that identifies the impacts of losing an organization's resources and measures the effect of resource loss and escalating losses over time.[5] Its purpose is to provide reliable data upon which to base decisions on mitigation, recovery, and business continuity strategies. It helps an organization establish the value of each business unit and business process as it relates to the organization, illustrating which functions need to be recovered and in what order.[6]

Organizational Resilience

Organizational resilience refers to the ability of an organization to recover from a crisis event. It depends upon the policies and procedures the organization has instituted and the support provided to staff, members, and attendees. Studies indicate that more than 40% of businesses seriously affected by disasters do not reopen, and of those that do, almost 30% close within three years.[7]

Post-Traumatic Stress Disorder

Talk to your staff and attendees about their thoughts, feelings, and fears regarding the incident. Many survivors not only deal with survivor guilt but also have post-traumatic stress disorder. Find out how they are handling the normal fears and guilt that often result from being a survivor of a violent incident. Not everyone will react in the same way.

If they do not want to talk to you, encourage them to talk to someone. Refer them to counseling as necessary.

Talk honestly about your own feelings regarding violence. It is important for people to recognize they are not dealing with their fears alone. Even those who were not at the facility during the incident will be dramatically affected.

Legal Action

Some victims of the event may sue the organization for failure to protect or for the mental anguish and physical trauma suffered as a result. People react differently to stressful incidents, so be prepared for even a longtime employee or attendee to sue.

Public Relations

In Chapter 12, we will discuss handling the media, who will almost certainly be involved if there is an incident. However, information that is provided to the media must be timely, accurate, and factual. Never engage in speculation.

Post-Incident Analysis and Evaluation

The post-incident analysis and evaluation is a critical step. This is where key players discuss the situation and how it was handled. It is just as important to discuss what went right as it is to discuss what went wrong. Any problems with the way the situation was handled or other concerns should be brought up and discussed.

The following questions should be asked to gauge the psychological recovery of your attendees:[8]

1. Could it have been handled better?
2. Were there any signs that were ignored?
3. Is counseling available for those who need it?
4. Is counseling being offered for those who think they don't need it?
5. Has there been a change in the attendance of those who have been exposed to the incident?
6. Has there been a change in the attitude of those who have been exposed to the incident?
7. Has there been a change in the behavior of those who have been exposed to the incident?
8. Has there been a change in the social interaction of those who have been exposed to the incident?

Record

Once the incident has passed, accurate documentation will allow you to evaluate your plans on their effectiveness in handling the situation. It also provides support for security recommendations and can even protect you from liability.

Revision of Policies

In many cases, policies and procedures will need to be revised to incorporate findings of the evaluation.

Your program will need to be continually updated to ensure it continues to meet the needs of your organization. This should be done annually at the very least. It should also be reviewed after every incident. A schedule for evaluation with assigned roles and responsibilities should be established to ensure the plan is reviewed and updated as necessary. Other reasons/times for evaluating and revising your plan(s) include whenever new technologies, policies, or procedures are adopted by the facility. In addition, high-profile events can serve as a catalyst for updating plans. Plans should also be updated with staff turnover. Changes should be documented with a revision date. Even if no changes are made, the evaluation date should be recorded.

Refresher Training

Once it has been determined what went right and what went wrong, staff and employees should be trained on changes in policies and procedures. Refresher training should also be conducted every few months to avoid complacency.

Long Term

Once immediate needs are taken care of, it is time to focus on the long-term aspects of recovery, reconstruction, and restoration. Some organizations never fully recover after a devastating incident. Staff and/or attendees may be too fearful to return to the location where they experienced trauma.

The recovery process must balance the immediate need to return the community to normal with the longer term goal of reducing future vulnerability.[8] However, some issues will not be revealed until after the disaster has occurred.

Psychological Recovery

Psychological needs as well as physical safety should also be addressed. There is an increased likelihood of the emergence of Acute Stress Disorder, Post-traumatic Stress Disorder, and depression as recovery efforts continue.[9] Some studies estimate that for every one physical casualty, there are 4–20 psychological victims.[10] As a result, organizations such as "nursing, human resources, and social work as well as the chaplaincy, organizational development, and mission staff should be included in mental health planning sessions."[11] Triage should be set up for the following groups of people: "survivors, those who lost loved ones, rescue workers, and people who witnessed the events; those who lost a home, business, or job; and anyone else who was deeply affected."[12]

Compassion Fatigue

The stress of working with populations in crisis can lead to compassion fatigue, secondary traumatic stress, vicarious traumatization, and burnout in those offering aid to victims.[13] Compassion fatigue describes the cumulative effects of working with traumatized individuals that contribute to secondary traumatic stress of the caregiver.[14] It is important to recognize the signs of compassion fatigue, which include cognitive, emotional, physical, spiritual, interpersonal, and behavioral reactions such as decreased level of concern and empathy for clients, decreased positive feeling for clients, physical and emotional exhaustion, increased levels of job dissatisfaction, and feelings of hopelessness related to the job.[15] It is of the utmost importance to include mental health care in emergency plans and to recognize those signs of stress, fatigue, and burnout in emergency personnel as well as victims.

Summary

Two of the main issues with recovery planning are locating and accessing resources and resuming normal activities.[16] Businesses and individuals should return to normal as soon as possible. This is not only important for the economic vitality of an organization, but for the psychological recovery as well.

Incident recovery can be a long and arduous process. Planners can only account for the basics, as a disaster will bring about many unforeseen events. In the end, a good emergency manager will be flexible enough to adapt plans as needed to the current situation.

End Notes

1. Alexander D. E., *Principles of Emergency Planning and Management* (New York: Oxford University Press, 2002), 5.
2. Alexander D. E., *Principles of Emergency Planning and Management* (New York: Oxford University Press, 2002).
3. ASIS Commission on Standards and Guidelines, *Business Continuity Guideline: A Practical Approach for Emergency Preparedness, Crisis Management, and Disaster Recovery* (Alexandria: ASIS, International, 2005).
4. Fischer R. J., Halibozek E. and Green G., *Introduction to Security*, Eighth Edition (Massachusetts: Butterworth-Heinemann, 2008).
5. See note 3 above.
6. Broder J. F., *Risk Analysis and the Security Survey*, Third Edition (Massachusetts: Elsevier Butterworth Heinemann, 2006).
7. McGlown K. J., *Terrorism and Disaster Management: Preparing Healthcare Leaders for the New Reality* (Chicago: Health Administration Press, 2004).
8. Haddow G. D., Bullock J. A. and Coppola D. P., *Introduction to Emergency Management*, Fourth Edition (Massachusetts: Butterworth-Heinemann, 2011).
9. Maiden R. P., Paul R. and Thompson C., eds., *Workplace Disaster, Preparedness, Response, and Management* (Haworth Press, 2006).
10. See note 7 above.
11. See note 7 above. p. 7.
12. See note 7 above. p. 7.

13. See note 9 above.
14. See note 9 above.
15. See note 9 above.
16. See note 7 above.

Handling the Media

12

Introduction

If an incident occurs at your facility or involves a prominent member of your organization, the media will likely become involved. Depending upon the type of incident, media interest could be local, national, or even international. In a rush to get the story first, initial media reports are often inaccurate. In addition, the media is often very quick to place blame even without any supporting facts.

Social media can also contribute to the rapid spread of misinformation and turn a local crisis into a national one. The 24-hour news cycle means that staff and attendees may receive information and misinformation before you do. You need to control the flow of information to protect the victims, aid in the investigation, and to comfort the rest of your attendees.

On the other hand, the media can be the best way to get accurate information out quickly to the public. This can help with investigation by generating leads and finding suspects. You can use the media to your advantage by cooperating with them and providing timely and accurate information for them to broadcast.

Cooperating with the media can also help you contain them. Containment refers to setting appropriate limits for media representatives and helps ensure that they will cover the story without excessive or gratuitous footage of carnage and/or mourning members.[1] You want them to help, not hinder investigation and recovery.

Media Liaison

The most important thing you can do is to have a designated spokesperson or media liaison. All media inquiries are forwarded to them, and they are the only ones authorized to make statements to the media. This person should be designated and trained before an incident occurs.

This does not have to be a hired media consultant. Anyone within your organization can be designated for this position. However, they should possess the characteristics of calm under pressure, trustworthiness, dependability, and sincerity. They should have the ability to speak clearly, concisely, and calmly. They do not have to be eloquent but should be easily understood.

They should be trained in how to deal with the various media outlets including social media formats, as information and misinformation can spread rapidly. They should be able to write key messages in a clear and concise format using only facts. They should avoid embellishments and speculation.

The media liaison should also monitor news reports to see what is being written about the incident and to correct any misinformation. They should have a prepared written statement to provide to any news outlets regarding the incident.

Staff and attendees should be instructed to provide no information about the incident to the media and to direct all inquiries to the designated spokesperson. They can use such phrases as "please leave me alone," "I do not want to talk," "No comment," or "Do not take my picture."[2] If possible, the spokesperson should have a dedicated phone number and email to address these concerns.

Media Policy

Prior to an incident occurring, a media policy should be established for staff and religious leaders. The policy should include, at a minimum, the following:

1. Designated spokesperson and contact information (you may want a dedicated email address or phone line)
2. Statement granting authority to the designated spokesperson to speak on behalf of the religious institution
3. What individuals are authorized to say
4. How decisions are made as to what the spokesperson will say
5. Designated backup spokesperson
6. How information will be disseminated to the media, i.e., written statements, radio or television interviews, newspaper editorials, online blogs, press conferences, Facebook updates, Twitter messages, Website updates, etc. You can use some or all of these methods, but be sure the message is consistent across all mediums.
7. It should also state that staff/attendees are not authorized to speak to the media about the incident and they are not allowed to post information regarding it to social media.
8. Include what is *not* to be disseminated to the media, such as names, photos, or other personal information about victims or suspects or names of potential witnesses or family and friends of victims or perpetrators.[3]

Media Statements

To get out in front of media speculation and control the narrative, the media liaison should issue a written statement to the media as soon as possible. The statement should contain a few key messages and be factually correct. There is no room for speculation.

---

1. Focus on facts.
2. Develop concise key messages.
3. Write in short, simple, clear sentences.
4. Have others review it.
5. Send to all interested media outlets.

As developments occur, additional statements can be issued provided they remain factual and do not hinder police investigations. As the situation continues to unfold, it may be necessary to hold a press conference. This is particularly appropriate if the story is gaining national attention.

Press Conferences

If the incident is attracting national and/or international attention, a press conference may be the best way to get information out to the public that is accurate, timely, and factual. This ensures that all media representatives receive the same information at the same time and from the same source.

Preparation

Prepare for the conference as you would any important speech. You want to be as factual, clear, and concise as possible. Avoid speculation on motives. In addition, do not provide personal information or photographs of victims or alleged perpetrators. Keep your statements focused on the facts.

Your message should focus on a few specific key messages. These can include safety, cooperating with the investigation, support services, and prevention of further incidents. Write it down and have others review it for clarity and accuracy. Rehearse it with someone playing the role of the reporters who will be asking you questions. This statement will not only be presented by you at the press conference, but it will also be provided to media outlets to ensure your message is received intact.

---

1. Focus on facts.
2. Develop key messages.
3. Write in short, simple, clear sentences.
4. Have others review it.
5. Rehearse it.
6. Have someone ask you questions.

Press Conference

You want to announce the time and location of the first press conference as soon as is practical. Make it clear that your facility will be cooperating with the media, but they are to leave your staff and attendees alone. Poland and McCormick (1999)[4] provide the following tips:

1. Begin by asking the media to hold all questions until the end.
2. Speak in short, clear, fact-filled sentences. Try to use phrases that quickly and clearly communicate your message and will be appropriate as "sound bites."
3. Always release information regarding safety first and, if accurate, that the situation has been contained.
4. Give known facts in a complete and truthful manner as any attempts to cover up information will result in loss of credibility.

5. Explain that you are cooperating with law enforcement who will provide additional details as they see fit. You do not want to release any information that will be detrimental to the investigation and prosecution.
6. Describe how you are fixing the problem and/or preventing future incidents.
7. Emphasize support being provided to affected people and use the media to dispense important information about assistance available to the community.
8. If applicable, emphasize that violence and/or crime is a societal problem and prevention involves a community-wide approach.

Answering the Media's Questions

After you have made your statement, the media will want you to answer questions and may request interviews. You should require that you be provided knowledge of the subject matter prior to granting interview requests.

Set the pace by taking the time you need to think clearly about your answers. You can do this by slowly repeating the question before you provide an answer. Do not allow yourself to be intimidated or pressured into providing immediate answers as this may cause you to blurt out inaccuracies. Answer only one question at a time and ignore interruptions.

Always speak as clearly and calmly as possible. You want to answer as directly as you are able to and stick to the facts. Overlong explanations or speculation can do more harm than good.

---

1. Repeat the question before giving your answer.
2. Answer only one question at a time.
3. Speak calmly and clearly.
4. Ignore interruptions.
5. Discuss only facts and do not speculate!

If a question confuses or disconcerts you, ask them to repeat it. If questions seem pushy, accusatory, or otherwise inappropriate, you have several options for handling them. The first is to simply ignore them and take another reporter's question. You can also rephrase them and answer them in a way that focuses on your key points. Or you can respond by stating something like "That's not what we need to focus on at this time" or "I'm sorry, I cannot provide that information."[5] Refer them to the law enforcement spokesperson for more information.

Aftermath

You must be prepared for the media to dig up negative information or portrayals of your facility.[6] You can proactively counter negative statements by addressing them and pointing out the facts. They may also try to draw comparisons with other incidents. Again, emphasize the facts and state that you refuse to engage in speculation without supporting evidence. This is known as spin control.

Another way to counter such speculation is to visit the editorial board of local papers within 48 hours to give your side of the story.[7] Remember to keep your message clear and consistent across all presentation mediums.

Follow-Up

Even if there is no new information to announce, continue holding press conferences every 2 to 3 h throughout the day. When there is no new information, emphasize policies and prevention programs and provide information about the crisis management steps that your facility is taking.[8] Also, remind the media that the police are conducting an ongoing investigation and you will not interfere with their job.

In the weeks and months that follow, the media may come back to document your facility's progress. In addition, they may return on the anniversary of the incident or when the alleged perpetrator goes to trial. If a similar incident occurs at another facility and captures the media attention, they may return to compare how the situations are handled. Regardless of why they return, you can still use the same ground rules you had for the initial media attention.

---

1. Do not allow them to film on the grounds of your facility.
2. Allow them to interview the media liaison but not staff and attendees.
3. Do not provide personal information about how victims are coping.

Other Considerations

The media can have a significant impact on your facility in many ways, not just during an incident or in the aftermath. Having a dedicated liaison can help establish a positive relationship with the media such as highlighting charitable works. Building rapport with media representatives can help reinforce the importance of privacy and confidentiality if and when an incident occurs.[9]

Perception of Crime

Numerous studies indicate that the media has a strong influence on how people view crime, the criminal justice system and the police, their fear of crime, and their opinions of punishments.[10] Studies show that news reports of local crimes increases fear of crime among the local population, whereas news of nonlocal crime increases feelings of safety.[11] This distorts the incidence of crime and influences which crimes we are prepared for and which we are not.

You do not want your attendees fearful and afraid to enjoy your facility. However, you do them and your staff a disservice by refusing to acknowledge criminal activity that has occurred at your facility. This creates a false sense of security that may lead to taking unnecessary risks such as failure to follow basic security procedures and general precautions. In addition, it can breed feelings of betrayal and distrust once the extent of criminal activity is revealed. People talk, and if someone is aware of an incident, soon the whole group may know. It is best to control the flow of information to prevent misinformation and fear.

You should be simple and direct when telling others of incidents. You do not have to provide extensive details. You should also tell them how to avoid becoming victims. Here are some examples:

1. We have had some thefts from cars in the parking lot during services. Please remember to hide your valuables, roll up your windows, and lock your doors.
2. There have been reports of robberies/assaults in the surrounding neighborhood. Please be sure to park in well-lit areas and pay attention to your surroundings as you walk to your vehicles. Have your keys in hand and immediately lock the doors once you are inside.
3. There have been reports of people loitering around the facility. Please remember to walk in pairs or groups and to report any suspicious individuals to law enforcement or the facility's designated contact.
4. Do not leave your purses or wallets unattended.

In addition, let them know to how to report suspicious behavior and who to report it to. Many people are reluctant to report suspicious behavior out of fear that they may be wrong. Assure them that the information will be evaluated and handled properly.

Manufactured Crises and Trends

The media, whether intentional or not, often distorts the reality of crime, often by making rare crimes seem to be common or even an epidemic.[12] The media can manufacture crises and report on "trends" that do not really exist. In 2001, there was an "epidemic" of alligator attacks, and 2002 saw a similar epidemic of shark attacks. The problem is that both of those years saw fewer attacks overall and fewer casualties compared with previous summers, but the media focused on the stories and exaggerated them far beyond the real dimensions of the situation.[13]

The problem with this is that it creates unnecessary fear. It can also lead to spending time, money, and other resources on preventing an incident that is very unlikely to happen. Not every attack on a religious institution is a hate crime committed by outsiders. The motivations and methods of attack are numerous. By focusing solely on outsiders, you run the risk of overlooking insiders who may wish to harm the institution itself, its employees, or its attendees. This prevents your facility from being adequately prepared for real threats by being overly focused on unlikely ones. Refer to Chapter 4 on Evaluating Risk for information on how to rank the likelihood of certain types of crime affecting your facility.

The Copycat Effect

It has been well documented that when a crime captures the public attention there is a brief increase in the number of similar crimes. As Loren Coleman states "Individual violent acts portrayed in the media tend to spawn similar incidents in the days and weeks that follow, though the subsequent events may be murder-suicides, mass murders, or mass suicides regardless of the precipitating event."[14] Angry and vulnerable people see these "successful" acts and try to emulate them.

As a result, if your facility, or one nearby, has been the victim of a publicized crime, it is reasonable to expect that you will receive additional threats of a similar nature. This is not to say crimes should not be publicized, as the attention can lead to quicker resolutions. However, it is a reminder that there may be a brief increase in the weeks and months that follow. Vigilance and preparation are critical.

It is important to remember that people make threats for a variety of reasons. Some people simply want attention, whereas others enjoy shocking people. It is difficult to judge people's motivations. As a result, all threats should be taken seriously and reported to local law enforcement and your security team.

Re-victimization and Re-traumatization

Another reason for controlling the flow of information is to prevent victims from being traumatized again by intrusive coverage. Watching reenactments can force survivors to relive the incident and further damage their fragile psyche. Many resent the media as intimidating and intrusive while they are trying to make sense of what happened. They view the media as violating them a second time.

As a result, you need to set ground rules for who, where, and when the media can access your facility. If necessary, you can have your security team, if you have one, or the police deny media access.

The media should not be allowed on the facility's grounds and definitely not inside it or near the crime scene.[15] They should not film injured or deceased attendees and staff or those in mourning. They should also refrain from asking painful questions of friends and family of victims, witnesses, and suspected perpetrators.[16]

To protect staff and attendees, you should deny the media access to any community or facility meetings so as to allow those affected time to process what has happened, to grieve, and to heal.[17] They do not need to be photographed, filmed, or interviewed during these difficult times. In a rush to get the best story or exclusive, the media can be insensitive to the suffering of victims.

Failure of the media to follow these rules should result in them being barred from press conferences. Be sure to inform them of your policy and to enforce it as necessary.

First Informers and Social Media

The rise of technology has led to the advent of "first informers." These are ordinary citizens with cell phones who are on the scene of an incident and provide some of the first images of the situation as it unfolds.[18]

While they can provide valuable information to law enforcement and to families looking for information on loved ones, they can also be intrusive and insensitive. They may contribute to the spread of rumor and misinformation, which can hinder relief efforts and investigations. This can be difficult to control, but you can begin by asking staff and attendees to be respectful and careful about what they share.

When an Attendee or Staff Member Commits a Crime

Unfortunately, sometimes a member of the staff or an attendee is the perpetrator of a crime, not a victim. This can put a bright spotlight on your religious institution as the media seeks to uncover any motivation or contributing factor to the crime. This can be very distressing to the attendees and staff as they will feel scrutinized for their beliefs and suffer guilt by association. If this occurs, a simple statement should be issued such as the following: "The alleged crimes are not condoned by our facility and in no way reflect our doctrine or the people who attend our facility. We have no further comment."

An individual does not have to commit a crime, but only be accused of one, to have the glare of the media focused on them. Again, a statement may need to be issued such as "We will not engage in speculation and will wait until the police conclude their investigation before commenting." As the individual may be falsely accused, you want to refrain from condemning them or slandering their name.

These are very difficult situations that must be considered and handled with extreme sensitivity. You will need to conduct damage control within your institution as well as within the surrounding community. You do not want to appear to be condoning criminal activity, but you do not want to rush to judgment should the accused actually be innocent.

Final Thoughts

The media can bring awareness to issues affecting the community, but they can also sensationalize an event. This can severely damage the people affected as well as the religious institution to which they belong. It is essential that you work with the media to ensure the information that is released is timely, factual, and accurate.

End Notes

1. Poland S. and McCormick J. S., *Coping with Crisis: A Quick Reference* (Colorado: Sopris West, 2000).
2. Ibid.
3. Ibid.
4. Poland S. and McCormick J. S., *Coping with Crisis: Lessons Learned* (Colorado: Sopris West, 1999).
5. Ibid.
6. Ibid.
7. Ibid.
8. Ibid.
9. Ibid.
10. Muraskin R. and Domash S. F., *Crime and the Media: Headlines vs. Reality* (New Jersey: Pearson Education, Inc., 2007).
11. Ibid.

12. Ibid.
13. Coleman L., *The Copycat Effect: How the Media and Popular Culture Trigger the Mayhem in Tomorrow's Headlines* (New York: Paraview Pocket Books, 2004).
14. Ibid, p. 135.
15. See note 4 above.
16. See note 4 above.
17. See note 4 above.
18. Haddow G. D., Bullock J. A. and Coppola D. P., *Introduction to Emergency Management*, Fourth Edition (Massachusetts: Butterworth-Heinemann, 2011).

Recognizing Intangible Capital and Liability Concerns

13

Losses that can occur to your organization are often more than loss of physical property or human life. In addition to tangible assets, there are many intangible assets that are also affected in the wake of an incident.

We mentioned this briefly in Chapter 4 on Evaluating Risk. However, it is time to delve a little deeper into how these assets can be affected by a security incident and other liability concerns.

Intangible Assets

Some intangible assets include the following:

1. Loss of sense of safety and security
2. Loss of reputation
3. Loss of relationships
4. Loss of trust

A loss of a sense of security can drive people away from the institution as can a loss of reputation of the facility as a safe place.

When religious leaders commit crimes, the damage to the facility's organization can be such that followers lose faith in their religion entirely. As a result, protecting intangible assets is just as important as protecting tangible ones such as property.

Intangible Capital

Intangible capital includes those components of an organization that affect its success but are not physical items. These include reputation, goodwill, and relationships within the community. These elements are essential to a successful organization of any kind. A bad reputation within the community will cause tension between your facility and those it tries to help.

Many religious institutions are reluctant to implement strong security measures for fear that members will feel threatened instead of protected and many congregants are uncomfortable with the idea of armed people in the facility.[1] According to ASIS research, "police officers who frequently attend church often leave their guns at home because they do not want to offend people at church who might think less of them for carrying weapons into the place of worship."[2] The church may fear losing members if it is considered unsafe, or it may fear alienating members if the perpetrator turns out to be an insider. Crime causes members to lose hope regardless of whether the perpetrator is a fellow member or an outsider. The church itself loses credibility. In extreme cases, victims or witnesses may question their faith.

Religious institutions may also fear retaliation, civil suits, and the possibility of additional people making similar allegations whether true or not. They may feel that incidents reflect poorly on the decision-making skills or piety of the leaders or members.[3] Unfortunately, some congregations split and other religious institutions close as a result of lawsuits, accusations, and the aftermath of traumatic events.[4]

Protecting Your Facility's Reputation

So how do you protect your facility from a loss of intangible capital? There are four stages to safeguarding and recovering reputation: rescue, rewind, restore, and recover.[5] Each stage is then broken down into steps.

Stage One: Rescue

The initial stage of rescue is to minimize the damage that has occurred after an incident. It involves the following four steps:[6]

1. Take the heat
2. Communicate tirelessly
3. Reset the company clock
4. Do not underestimate your critics and competitors

When an incident occurs, first and foremost, leaders need to take responsibility for managing the incident and demonstrating empathy and sincerity for those affected in the crisis. This includes being the official spokesperson. Communication must be timely, transparent, and proactive.[7] Leaders should act quickly to communicate what is happening and how they are trying to rectify the situation. Refer back to Chapter 12 for more information on communication with the media.

Although no one likes to be criticized, critics may be telling you something you do not want to hear but need to consider.[8] Critics do not go away if they are ignored. If it appears you are not responding properly to concerns, you can alienate your members as well.

Resetting the clock refers to deciding what happens next instead of focusing on what went wrong.[9] Do not waste time with regret and recriminations, but work to move forward.

Stage Two: Rewind

The rewind stage is identifying what went wrong and includes two steps.[10]

1. Analyze what went wrong and right
2. Measure, measure, and measure again

Once a course of action has been decided upon, the organization needs to analyze what went wrong. However, they should not focus solely on problems. They should also consider what went right.

After the analysis of strengths and weaknesses, it is time to decide on how to measure progress with real-time hard evidence that the organization is moving in the right direction.[11] Stakeholders are anyone who has an interest in the organization including attendees, staff, those who use the organization's services, and potential members. Some questions to consider are the following:[12]

1. What do we want stakeholders to believe about us?
2. What do stakeholders believe about us now?
3. What did stakeholders believe about us before the crisis?
4. What is the gap between how we want to be perceived and how we are perceived now?
5. How do we communicate with internal and external stakeholders?
6. Which of our messages resonate and are credible?
7. Which messages need clarification, amplification, or adjustment?
8. How do stakeholders learn about us?

Stage Three: Restore

The restore stage is for rebuilding reputation after an incident and has three steps:[13]

1. Right the culture
2. Seize the shift
3. Brave the media

Righting the culture can be the most difficult aspect, but it is crucial. In many cases, systemic issues are the vulnerabilities and weaknesses of an organization. Without a change of the culture, the problems will likely keep occurring. This can be accomplished by making recovery values-based; hiring the correct personnel and using the right volunteers; reaffirming people's belief in themselves; and identifying common purpose and values.[14]

Seizing the shift involves changing business models, practices, and operational procedures as needed to keep up with social, business, or political changes. This can be particularly difficult for religious institutions that rely heavily on tradition. This does not mean you have to change your fundamental belief system to follow fads, but you need to be aware of how opinions shift and the impact it can have on your organization.

The final step in this stage concerns dealing with the media. We discussed this in Chapter 12. However, it concerns the long-term use of the media to build and strengthen your reputation. This includes letting the media know of charity events and other community outreach without being self-aggrandizing. Remaining humble and sincere is important to building and maintaining your reputation.

Stage Four: Recover

The recovery stage is concerned with sustaining your reputation long term and has three steps.[15]

1. Build a drumbeat of good news
2. Commit to a marathon, not a sprint
3. Minimize reputation risk

One of the most important things to realize is that "recovering reputation typically does not come from one major event or announcement, but rather from a series of small incremental steps that slowly generate positive momentum."[16] Ways to do this are to keep your message simple and straightforward, use symbolic acts, and make signs of progress visible.[17]

It may only take one incident to destroy a reputation, but rebuilding it takes a great deal of time and effort. This is the essence of committing to a marathon.

Finally, you can minimize reputation risk. This is everyone's responsibility. Two ways to do this are to stay ahead of the curve and plan for the worst-case scenario.[18] Chapter 4 on evaluating risk will show you how to plan.

Liability Concerns

Religious institutions also need to be aware of liability issues that can affect the facility. While state and local liability laws may differ, there are some basic ways that liability can be attached to the facility and its users. The most common of these are property liability and liability resulting from employees and/or volunteers.

Property liability includes unsafe conditions. Liability can also be attached if someone is the victim of a crime on facility grounds and can show that security was inadequate to protect them or prevent the incident.

The first step is to ensure you are aware of local, state, and federal laws and regulations that can affect your facility. This includes Occupational Safety and Health Act (OSHA) standards and regulations for a safe work environment.

Additional liability issues include the following:

- Negligent hiring, negligent training, negligent supervision, negligent retention, and negligent recommendation or misrepresentation[19]
- Sexual misconduct or harassment
- Breach of contract[20]
- Premises liability[21]
- Defamation of character including libel and slander
- Causing emotional distress either intentionally or through negligence[22]
- Inadequate supervision of children and youth
- Breach of fiduciary responsibility
- Invasion of privacy
- Wrongful termination of employee
- Failure to warn
- Criminal liability for failing to protect abused children and prevent future abuse[23]
- Failure to take reasonable steps to prevent discrimination and harassment
- Fraud
- Breach of statutory duty[24]
- Malpractice or negligent counseling[25]
- Use of property by outside groups[26]

Business Impacts of Violence

Violent incidents have several negative impacts on an organization. These include downtime, loss of workforce, loss of customer goodwill, falling productivity per employee, public relations and media impact, cost of increased security, cost of the investigation, legal costs, and employee assistance.[27] Although they use business terminology, they are applicable to religious institutions as employees and volunteers are your workforce, and your customers are members, attendees, and those who use your outreach services.

Reducing Liability

There are a variety of things you can do to reduce your liability, including the following:

1. Use safe hiring practices including criminal background checks and checking references.
2. Use screening practices for volunteers, particularly if they are working with children and youth.
3. Educate staff and volunteers on risks associated with their positions.
4. Have an attorney who specializes in religious institution law conduct liability and responsibility training.[28]
5. Let volunteers know that their actions could result in liability to the religious institution.
6. Conduct random checks of organizational activities and assess the level of risk.[29]
7. Post instructions and procedures in visible places.[30]
   a. Location of exits
   b. Use of kitchen and other facilities
   c. Use of equipment
   d. Location of safety equipment such as fire extinguishers and first aid kits
   e. Accident response procedures
8. Educate staff and volunteers on policies.
9. Enforce noncompliance with established policies and procedures.

Protecting Your Facility from Lawsuits

One devastating effect of liability incidents is the possibility of lawsuits. Without a risk management program, the institution is more susceptible to having judgments against them. A few recent cases are given as follows:

- New York: A jury awarded $11.45 million to two teens who were sexually molested by the church's youth minister.[31]
- Missouri: A church was sued after five youth drowned in a river during a church outing.[32]
- Ohio: A jury awarded $5.76 million in damages after a young boy was spanked by a teacher in the church day care.[33]
- Maryland: A female church music director was awarded $1.35 million after being sexually harassed by the pastor.[34]

The Pew Forum's 2011 report on the legal status of religious organizations in civil lawsuits divided the court cases into four types: property disputes; employment of clergy; treatment or discipline of members; and misconduct by employees of religious organizations.[35]

Lawsuits cost money to defend against and legal costs are unlikely to be recouped even if you win the case. It costs a plaintiff little money to sue a religious institution as cases are often taken on a contingency-fee basis.[36] Lawsuits by their own members are on the rise for issues such as negligence, poor supervision of children and youth, unsafe facilities, and improper counseling.[37]

The religious institution can be held liable for the actions of anyone who is involved in an official capacity in an activity under the authority and knowledge of the facility or its leaders.[38]

What Can You Do?

The best way to handle a lawsuit is to prevent it from ever happening. Prevention activities include the following:

1. Conducting a risk assessment
2. Implementing a risk management program
3. Instituting security countermeasures
4. Establishing policies and procedures
5. Training and retraining your staff and volunteers
6. Ensuring proper supervision of volunteers, staff, and activities
7. Regular evaluations and updates of policies and procedures
8. Enforce compliance with policies and procedures by following through on consequences for noncompliance.

You also need to be prepared to respond to lawsuits.

1. Do not panic and be sure to consider your response carefully before taking action.
2. Do not assume a member who is also a lawyer will become the legal counsel for the organization. However, they may be able to point you in the right direction to get legal help.
3. Research attorneys to make sure you engage one that has specific experience in dealing with law concerning religious organizations.
4. Interview lawyers for their fee schedule, mind-set, qualifications, understanding of religious organization law, and potential conflicts of interest.[39]
5. Set aside organizational funds for legal matters.[40]
6. Educate your legal counsel on organizational policies, bylaws, activities, and structures.[41]
7. Be open to legal advice on areas in need of change.[42]
8. Consider having personal attorneys for each leader as an organizational attorney may have a conflict of interest if litigation is between members of the facility.[43]

Insurance

As mentioned in Chapter 4 on Evaluating Risk, insurance does not remove the religious institution's responsibility for reducing risk, and it does not prevent incidents from happening. Nevertheless, insurance is needed, including liability coverage for the following[44]:

1. Commercial general
2. Pastoral professional
3. Directors and officers
4. Employment practices
5. Owned automobile
6. Hired and non-owned automobile
7. Umbrella
8. Leader's personal

Be aware that insurance may not cover all of the costs of a lawsuit as policies have liability limits and exclusions. Make sure that your insurance policies are tailored to the specific needs of your institution. Ensure you understand what your policies do and do not cover. Update them as necessary.

Final Thoughts

Reputation wounds are often self-inflicted such as financial irregularities, unethical behavior, and executive misconduct.[45] These issues can be prevented with appropriate security measures such as risk management strategies, established policies and procedures, and liability training.

Reputation is extremely important. It can affect not only the members of your organization, but any attempts at community outreach as well. Unfortunately, an incident at an institution of the same denomination or tradition can have far-reaching consequences for your organization and others. Critics are quick to seize one incident as evidence that a particular religion is bad or corrupt. You can minimize reputation erosion by facing issues head-on and proactively taking control of a situation with sincerity and accountability. If an incident occurs at another facility of the same denomination or tradition, you can highlight to your attendees how your particular organization is prepared to prevent and respond to a similar situation.

There are a multitude of liability issues as well that must be prepared for and protected against. In an increasingly litigious society, the likelihood of your facility or leaders being sued is certainly a possibility. Insurance can offer some protection, but a risk management program is essential to reducing vulnerability. One part of this is security awareness training, which is covered in the next chapter.

End Notes

1. Quarles and Ratliff, 2001.
2. Quarles and Ratliff, p. 4.
3. See note 1 above.
4. Hanna J. W., *Safe and Secure: The Alban Guide to Protecting Your Congregation* (Herndon: Alban Institute, 1999).
5. Gaines-Ross L., *Corporate Reputation: 12 Steps to Safeguarding and Recovering Reputation* (Hoboken: John Wiley & Sons, 2008).
6. Ibid.
7. Ibid.
8. Ibid.
9. Ibid.
10. Ibid.
11. Ibid.
12. See note 5 above, p. 89.
13. Ibid.
14. Ibid.
15. Ibid.
16. See note 5 above, p. 127.
17. Ibid.
18. Ibid.

19. Kerr K. M., *Workplace Violence* (Boston: Butterworth-Heinemann, 2010).

20. The GuideOne Center for Risk Management, *The Missing Ministry: Safety, Risk Management, and Protecting Your Church* (Loveland: The GuideOne Center for Risk Management, LLC, 2008).

21. Cobble Jr. J. F. and Hammar R. R., *Risk Management Handbook for Churches and Schools* (Matthews: Christian Ministry Resources, 2001).

22. See note 20 above.

23. See note 21 above.

24. The GuideOne Center for Risk Management, *The Missing Ministry: Safety, Risk Management, and Protecting Your Church* (Loveland: Group Publishing, Inc., 2008).

25. See note 21 above.

26. See note 21 above.

27. See note 19 above.

28. Hanna J. W., *Safe and Secure: The Alban Guide to Protecting Your Congregation* (Durham: Alban Institute, 1999).

29. Ibid.

30. Ibid.

31. See note 24 above.

32. See note 24 above.

33. See note 24 above.

34. See note 24 above.

35. http://www.pewforum.org/files/2011/03/Pillar_Autonomy.pdf.

36. See note 24 above.

37. See note 24 above.

38. See note 28 above.

39. See note 28 above.

40. See note 28 above.

41. See note 28 above.

42. See note 28 above.

43. See note 28 above.

44. See note 28 above.

45. See note 5 above.

Increasing Security Awareness 14

People are the most important component of effective security. It does not matter how effective a physical security system is if a person allows a perpetrator to enter the facility. The most important factor is getting people thinking about security whether they are employees, staff, volunteers, or attendees. This chapter focuses on basic security awareness, how to assess people's knowledge, how to train them, and how to maintain security awareness.

One of the greatest hurdles to effective security is a lack of security awareness. It is important that all employees, volunteers, and members are aware of simple security principles and procedures. In addition, they must be informed of policies and procedures of the facility as well. All of the latest access control technology will not do any good if it is not used properly.

Security awareness involves being cognizant of what is happening around you, how that information affects security now and in the future, and what you can do maintain security for yourself, your facility, information, and those around you. It is closely tied to situational awareness, which is defined as "the perception of the elements in the environment within a volume of time and space, the comprehension of their meaning, and the projection of their status in the near future."[1] Security awareness is recognizing the activities and behaviors that can negatively or positively impact security of individuals, information, facilities, and equipment. It should be the foundation for decision-making, risk management, development of policies and procedures, training, and performance.

Security awareness, like situational awareness, involves three steps: perception, comprehension, and projection.[2] Perception involves recognizing the status, attributes, and dynamics of elements in the environment that can impact security.[3] Environmental data is gathered through the five senses and can involve any combination of them. It can also involve verbal and nonverbal communication. An example is seeing two strangers in the facility who are wearing long coats despite the summer heat and watching the collection of money instead of the service.

Comprehension involves understanding how those elements can affect your security. Comprehension includes recognizing that those individuals, who likely have concealed weapons, are not interested in attending services at your facility.

Projection is the ability to predict what those elements will do in the short-term future. In our example, this means recognizing that the two strangers plan on robbing the institution. Understanding the three steps allows you to respond appropriately.

Factors that Negatively Affect Awareness

Maintaining security awareness can be difficult for a number of reasons as described by Endsley and Jones (2012)[4]:

1. Attentional tunneling: Focusing on processing certain aspects of the environment, results in intentionally or inadvertently stopping scanning and processing different information sources.
2. Requisite memory trap: Your memory bank has insufficient space to hold enough pertinent information.
3. Workload, anxiety, fatigue, and other stressors: These conditions can negatively impact your ability to effectively gather, process, and use information.
4. Data overload: "The rapid rate at which data changes creates a need for information intake that quickly outpaces the ability of a person's sensory and cognitive system."[5]
5. Misplaced salience: Occurs when your attention is drawn to distracting information and not the critical and highly important information needed to make appropriate decisions.[6] Criminals may use this to their advantage by creating a diversion or distraction.
6. Complexity creep: This refers to technology that has so many features that it is difficult for people to form sufficient internal representations of how the system works. This is can make it difficult to get the right technology for the job or to gauge its effectiveness.
7. Errant mental models: They are an incomplete mental model of "how to combine disparate pieces of information, how to interpret the significance of that information, and how to develop reasonable projections of what will happen in the future."[7]
8. Out-of-the-loop syndrome: This is mistakenly believing that automated systems are working as they should and, therefore, misunderstanding the state of the elements that the automated system is supposed to be controlling.

It is important to recognize these factors in order to try to control them and ensure that you make the proper decision based on accurate information.

Security Awareness Program

An effective security awareness program follows these steps:

1. Assess current understanding
2. Design training program
3. Implement training
4. Evaluate effectiveness
5. Maintain knowledge and skills

Assessing current understanding can be accomplished through quizzes and questionnaires regarding policies and procedures as well as basic security concepts. Then a training program is designed based on the security concepts, policies, and procedures relevant to your institution. If you have a small number of people to train, you can tailor the program to their individual needs.

To evaluate the effectiveness of the training, the easiest thing to do is to periodically quiz them on policies, procedures, and basic security concepts. It is important that you do not use the same questions as you want to check their understanding. Scenario questions are the most effective for they show an individual how to apply the information to a real situation they may encounter.

General Security Awareness

General security awareness techniques can be applied wherever you are and to almost whatever you are doing. Refer to your risk assessment to familiarize yourself with the vulnerabilities of your facility and potential threats.

Security awareness also involves looking strategically at your facility to look for potential vulnerabilities. Evaluate all areas where people can be. You should always be aware of potential hazards and what to do next if you encounter them. Christensen (2008) describes several questions to help you look at your facility strategically.[8]

1. Exits
   a. How many are near where you are right now?
   b. Where are they?
   c. What is on the other side of each door?
   d. Can the doors be locked?
   e. Can they be fortified with chairs, cabinets, or lockers?
   f. Do they have windows? Curtains?
   g. Where are the doors in every location you frequent during your day?
2. Hiding places
   a. Where can individuals hide?
      - How many can hide in each place?
      - Is it obvious someone is hiding there?
   b. Where can perpetrators hide?
   c. Is there a safe room?
3. Communication
   a. How do you let others know what is happening?
   b. Is there a way to contact security and/or law enforcement no matter where you are?
      - Silent duress alarms?
      - Landline phones?
      - Cell phones?
      - Public address system?
      - Other methods?

In order to appropriately respond to an incident, you need to have an idea of the potential dangers of your room space including doors, walls, and windows. Some elements you need to consider are the following[9]:

1. Door(s)
   a. How many?
   b. Do they open in or out? If it opens into a room, it can be barricaded to prevent access by an assailant.
   c. Can they be locked?
   d. Strong enough to survive a kick?

    e. Set into the frame or easily removed?
    f. Is there a window in it?
       - Large enough for someone to crawl through?
       - Shatterproof glass?
       - Is it close to the locking mechanism, so breaking it will allow someone to unlock the door?

2. Walls
    a. Thick enough to withstand kicking?
    b. Retractable?
    c. Soundproof?

3. Windows
    a. Location
    b. Glass
       - Is it break-resistant?
       - Are there objects you can use to break it if necessary?
    c. Size
       - Large enough for individuals to enter or exit through them?
    d. Tinted
       - Can you see into them from the outside?

Regardless of where people are located, you should also evaluate the following areas[10]:

1. Is there a predetermined holding/meeting area?
    a. What hazards exist in and around the holding areas?
    b. Are individuals aware of any secondary plans in case they cannot make it to designated holding areas?
    c. Are there incidents in which they will not report to holding areas?

2. Common areas/playgrounds
    a. What is the quickest route of escape?
    b. What areas of cover/protection and concealment/hiding are near or around these areas?
    c. Can the area be secured?

3. Grounds
    a. Where are safe areas to congregate and account for others?
    b. What are the communication methods with other areas?

4. Common areas: These include, for example, woods, dumpsters, or other areas of concealment where an individual or an improvised explosive device (IED) could be hidden from view and deployed. You should also be aware of these areas to relocate individuals in order to hide or provide cover for them.

5. Off-site trips
    a. How are individuals accounted for?
    b. How do you communicate danger to them to prevent them from returning to the site?

Another aspect of security awareness is to evaluate the vulnerabilities associated with activities. Consider the following questions:

1. Are individual staff members or volunteers alone at any time?
2. Are doors locked during off hours or at night?
3. What are the access control methods?

4. Is there a key control system?
5. What type of supervision is used for each activity?
6. How are staff/volunteers screened and trained?
7. Do others use the facilities for non-institution-related activities?

Personal Safety Tips

Security awareness training should include topics on personal safety. The following are suggested tips to increase personal security.

1. Always be aware of your surroundings.
2. Know where the nearest exits are located wherever you are.
3. Walk like you know where you are going and what you are doing, i.e., head up, eyes looking straight ahead, erect confident posture, and scan the area.
4. Do not unlock your car with electric keys until you are at the door.
5. Lock your car doors immediately upon getting into your vehicle.
6. Trust your instincts.
7. Visualize and practice appropriate responses to various situations.[11]
8. Know locations of telephones and first aid kits.
9. If you feel you are being harassed, threatened, or intimidated, tell them to stop and document the behavior.[12]
10. Lock doors and computers when you leave, even if only for a few minutes.
11. Lock valuables such as purses or electronic devices in a safe place.
12. Use the buddy system at night when walking to your car.
13. Institute a clean desk policy to ensure that confidential or proprietary information is not left in plain view but is locked up instead.
14. Do not touch suspicious items. Contact law enforcement and keep others away from the area.
15. Do not leave windows open or unlocked, especially those on the ground floor.
16. Do not prop doors open, even if you are "coming right back."
17. If you notice open doors or windows, close and lock them before proceeding cautiously. Have your cell phone pre-dialed to 911 in case you need to call for help.
18. Quickly scan the area before entering or exiting the facility to ensure there is no one loitering.
19. Do not sit with your back to the door, if possible. If you must sit with your back to the door, hang a mirror so you can see who is approaching.

Final Thoughts

Security awareness involves everything we have discussed so far from evaluating risk to understanding typical crimes and basic security concepts to choosing security countermeasures. It concerns understanding the clues in your environment to ensure you respond appropriately to potential danger.

You may want to have security professionals or law enforcement conduct training courses on personal safety including self-defense. This will not only provide valuable tips, but will increase confidence as well.

End Notes

1. Endsley M. R. and Jones D. G., *Designing for Situation Awareness: An Approach to User-Centered Design*, Second Edition (Boca Raton: CRC Press, 2012), 13.
2. Endsley M. R. and Jones D. G., *Designing for Situation Awareness: An Approach to User-Centered Design*, Second Edition (Boca Raton: CRC Press, 2012).
3. Ibid.
4. Ibid.
5. Ibid, p. 35.
6. Ibid.
7. Ibid, p. 39.
8. Christensen L. W., *Surviving a School Shooting: A Plan of Action for Parents, Teachers, and Students* (Boulder: Paladin Press, 2008).
9. Ibid.
10. Ibid.
11. Philpott D. and Grimme D., *The Workplace Violence Prevention Handbook* (Maryland: Government Institutes, 2009).
12. Ibid.

Implementing and Training

15

Once security countermeasures have been decided upon, implementation is the next step. This chapter focuses on how to present your security recommendations to leaders whose support you need in order to proceed, and to staff and volunteers who need to follow the recommendations, and what to tell and not to tell the congregation.

Training is vital in every aspect of security implementation, including policies and procedures, how to properly use equipment, how to handle incidents, how to report incidents, etc. In Chapter 14, we discussed security awareness training. This chapter focuses primarily on the training of staff and volunteers on policies and procedures.

Implementing a Security Program

A security program is necessary to protect your facility. It involves planning countermeasures and establishing policies and procedures for the facility's activities. Implementing a security program involves the following activities:

1. Ensure you have support from all of those within the organization that have authority to make decisions.
2. Conduct and periodically update the self-assessment of crime problems and needs of the community and organization.[1]
3. Identify goals and objectives.
4. Develop policies and procedures based on the security program.
5. Designate working groups and responsibilities for implementation.[2]
6. Provide oversight to implementation activities.
7. Evaluate progress and develop remedial action as necessary.
8. Manage the process with the following activities:
   a. System design and planning
   b. Coordination
   c. Training
   d. Assistance
   e. Monitoring
9. Define evaluation criteria of success.

Training

Training is vital in every aspect of security from policies and procedures to how to properly use equipment. Not only does it show them what to do and how to do it, it allows them to practice their tasks in a safe environment. In simulations, they can try different options and approaches, ask questions, and receive feedback from instructors. Training can also prevent personnel from inadvertently increasing the security risk.

The type of training depends on the individual's responsibilities, as it may simply be education at the awareness level or may include detailed operations or technician training.[3] It is also dependent on the individual's style of learning. Regardless of the type, it should be competency based, measurable, and include both initial and ongoing or refresher training.[4]

Prior to conducting training, an assessment based on current and desired competencies should be conducted.[5] This will allow you to ascertain what is needed in the training program and who needs it. Additional assessments should be conducted after training to ensure knowledge and skills were acquired with the desired level of proficiency.

Training can be conducted in several ways. However, academic, professional, and practical are three main methods.[6] Theoretical or academic is the most traditional form, such as typical classroom instruction.[7] To make it more practical and applicable to unpredictable situations, the lecture should be supplemented with hands-on training such as the use of equipment and software.[8] The American Heart Association's first aid and cardio pulmonary resuscitation (CPR) training uses video demonstrations, but it also offers opportunities for practice of rescue breathing, bandaging, helping a choking victim, and CPR with or without an automated external defibrillator (AED). This gives students a chance to practice the necessary skills. Evaluation by an instructor verifies that they learned the necessary information.

Participatory activities and exercises can include presentations by trainees, group discussions, and interactive computer software.[9] Personal and group research exercises, which lead to the preparation of reports, can be even more effective.[10] Hands-on training with equipment or software shows the practical application of knowledge and is a very effective training method.[11]

One dilemma in teaching courses is that no single teacher is likely to have the knowledge and experience to teach all aspects in a comprehensive course.[12] A variety of instructors can be useful, but they may make the training fragmented and incoherent.[13] In addition, they are likely to have differing teaching methods, meaning some may not be as effective as others.

Training should be divided into two main categories: general training and job-specific training. General training can be for employees, volunteers, and attendees. It is concerned with general security awareness and security policies. It should include recognizing suspicious behaviors, identifying vulnerabilities, and reporting of this information to the appropriate personnel.

Role-specific training should be only for the group that performs that specific job. For example, only those that handle the money should know the security policies and procedures for doing so. This will also avoid confusion during an emergency as individuals will know what they should do and not assume someone else is handling it. It will also reduce the possibility that people interfere with each other by trying to perform the same task in different ways.

Incident Management Training

Training courses should be designed for the phases of incident management—mitigation, preparedness, response, and recovery. Roles, responsibilities, and actions change depending upon the type of incident and what phase it is in. Prevention training is the most important. However, mitigation, response, and recovery training are also important.

It is important to not only assign roles but to have backups assigned in case an individual is unavailable or unwilling to handle a specific task. Remember—no matter how perfect your plans are, they cannot be executed without people who are available and properly trained.[14]

Students should be taught how to choose, combine, and implement mitigation techniques and methods.[15] Many of the potential losses of life and other damages can be avoided through sound mitigation techniques. Learning to design, write, implement, and test emergency operations plans and warning systems is essential for effective response and long-term recovery.

Training in crisis response teaches individuals to manage the early phases of emergencies. This is when individuals are taught the tasks and responsibilities of their previously assigned roles during an emergency. If they practice these tasks prior to an actual event, they are more likely to remember how to do it when needed and are more comfortable actually doing it. In a crisis situation, there is little time to think, but repeated practice will make it second nature. In addition, "employees at all levels need to be aware of and active participants in the continuity efforts of the entire organization, understanding the critical importance of their own flexibility in responding to varied scenarios, under a variety of circumstances, and possibly from a variety of different venues."[16]

Finally, training for the recovery phase focuses on reconstruction and repair.[17] Evaluations, critiques, and corrective actions are critical to the overall success or failure of future response and can be conducted through training or after real events.[18] Repair refers to not only physical construction but repairing the psychological and emotional wounds of the staff and attendees. The recovery and reconstruction phase can be the most difficult as it requires long-range planning in order to be most effective. If planners are shortsighted, their "quick fixes" may result in more damage in the long run.

Training Methods

Exercises offer important insight into response and recovery methods. They can be either tabletop exercises or field simulations.[19] They are an excellent method for testing plans, policies, procedures, and personnel.[20] They teach the vital components of timing, coordination, communication, roles, and responsibilities.[21] However, large-scale field tests are often expensive and difficult to conduct.

Three basic emergency management curriculum models can be used in crisis management training courses. These are the traditional cause-and-effect model, a more modern and adventurous concept-based approach (also known as the key-themes model), and scenario-based methods.[22]

The cause-and-effect model relies upon a linear progression from causes to impacts to responses.[23] It begins with a review of basic concepts then progresses to threat analysis, which is divided into categories based on natural, technological, and social agents.[24] Natural agents are natural disasters such as floods, hurricanes, and damaging winds. Technological agents involve hacking, phishing, and other computer hazards. Social agents involve criminal activity and perpetrators of hate crimes.

Special topics can be added to include coping with stress and a general survey of sociological and psychological aspects of disaster.[25] Its advantage is that it is straight-forward and well-organized. However, it is least conducive to innovative teaching methods.[26] It can also be difficult for some individuals to learn in this manner.

The concept-based approach is structured around key components of emergency management.[27] It links key terms—including hazard, vulnerability, risk, exposure, prediction, forecasting, warning, technology, planning, evacuation, management, logistics, and scenario construction—with related skills.[28] This approach is good at emphasizing the complexity of disasters and the need for interdisciplinary solutions and coordination.[29]

Scenario-based methods bridge the gap between abstract classroom instruction and practical training during real disasters.[30] Scenarios can be used as a basis for formu-lating security and response plans, "as the scenario indicates the amount and nature of resources needed to combat the hazard and how they must be deployed."[31] Scenarios are a means of testing students' abilities to respond effectively to practical problems and should be used to screen applicants for courses and to test their knowledge at the end of the training.[32] This methodology can also illustrate the limitations of particular situations, as well as the strengths and weaknesses of plans.[33]

Scenarios are flexible and induce participants to think of the consequences of their decisions and actions.[34] Typical scenarios provide a basic disaster situation and assign roles and tasks to participants.[35] The basic building blocks include the nature of the disaster impact, ground rules, logistical factors, roles of participants, objectives, and complicating factors or setbacks.[36]

During scenario training, updates and additional information can be provided, which either introduce change or provide information that was withheld at the out-set.[37] This makes the situation more realistic as first responders will not immediately have all of the facts on a disaster. In addition, disasters can lead to unanticipated cascading effects that will alter priorities and response procedures. Conflict and medi-ation can also be incorporated into disaster scenarios.[38] Realism is added by creating a less-than-optimal situation in which things do not go as planned.[39] Skills can be taught in addition to decision-making, thereby making scenarios a broadly applicable strategy for training in emergency management.

Scenarios are easily integrated with other forms of modeling and simulations, giv-ing them considerable potential for further development.[40] There are other methods correlated with scenarios. Case studies enable students to provide in-depth analyses of events or situations.[41] Case discussions can teach individuals how to analyze strengths and weaknesses in response and discover ways the incident could have been prevented.

One of the goals of simulation is for the student to determine the appropri-ate response for individual events, as a moderate event would require a different reaction than a severe one. These simulations should include a set of victims to train responders to identify severity and administer the appropriate corresponding level of intervention.

Computer simulations are another method that utilizes scenarios to present training. Scenario software programs are a great training aid as many of the unexpected and unique variables involved in real-life response can be easily simulated in software programs. They present as realistic a situation as possible that allows individuals to make decisions without involving real risk to themselves or others.[42] Not only can scenarios present different types of incidents, they exhibit varying levels of damages. Computer software provides the hands-on experience that is so vital to learning how to respond to different events. However, it can be difficult to find the most appropriate program and very costly to have one designed specifically for your facility.

Various types of exercises are orientation or information, tabletop, functional, and full scale.[43] Orientation exercises provide new staff with an overview of an organization's responsibilities, policies, procedures, and methods.[44] Tabletop exercises clear up any misunderstandings of responsibilities, capabilities, and methodologies while allowing personnel to become acquainted and collaborate effectively.[45] Using realistic threats in a regular tabletop exercise can improve decision-making and coordination. Refer to your risk assessment to make the situations as applicable to your specific facility as possible.

Functional exercises are operational and test specific elements of response such as communications, decontamination procedures, or resource distribution.[46] They are an effective way to test strengths and weaknesses in established procedures so they can be updated if necessary prior to a real disaster. Full-scale exercises are expensive, labor-intensive, and likely to interfere with normal operations.[47] Despite these drawbacks, they provide an unequaled opportunity to see how all elements function together as well as providing realistic and valuable training to all participants.[48] An important thing to remember with exercises or other scenarios is "if your exercise reveals nothing wrong, something is wrong with your exercise."[49] The goal of this training is to identify weaknesses and areas of improvement.

Current trends in disaster training include distance learning and online courses. These can incorporate lecture with simulations and interactive activities. The Federal Emergency Management Agency (FEMA) offers a variety of free courses online on emergency management topics including active shooter response at www.FEMA.gov.

Another type of training that is becoming popular is the train-the-trainer course.[50] "The purpose of the Train-the-Trainer courses are to develop a cadre of trainers who can raise awareness in their own localities."[51] In these courses, an individual is trained as an instructor in certain topics. They can then return to their company and train more individuals. This is often cost-effective as only one person is paying to take the training, and then they can teach innumerable employees what they learned. Many schools, my company included, take advantage of train-the-trainer programs. These programs utilize various methods of teaching and ensure that the students are effective teachers themselves. Many also provide any resource material needed to conduct classes. The first aid and CPR instructor courses taught through the American Heart Association are good examples.

Designing a Training Program

Everyone needs training on new policies and procedures, which can seem a daunting task. To make it more palatable and, therefore, more likely to be successful, you should focus on one type of training at a time. Prioritize the topics that need to be trained.

The effectiveness of your training program depends upon what you're trying to convey, your audience, and how you communicate the information. You have several options for training. You can choose the best option based on your target audience and the information you are trying to deliver. Using a combination of methods may work best to reinforce training and ensure that students truly understand the information.

Modeling

Modeling allows one to investigate situations safely and efficiently through trial and error. Good models are flexible enough so that changes in basic assumptions can lead to changes in outcomes.[52] The three main kinds of models are conceptual, physical, and numerical or digital.[53] The type that is used depends upon what you are trying to evaluate or show.

With modeling, it is important to recognize that bad input data generates bad or unreliable outputs. This means data must be as accurate as possible in order to generate useful models. One must also note the difference between variables, parameters, and constants in order for modeling to conduct an effective analysis.[54]

Scenarios

Scenarios are an interactive model of conditions and circumstances used to illustrate the connection between how conditions influence circumstances and how circumstances alter conditions.[55] They involve running through a likely situation with everyone performing their assigned roles. This allows them to practice in a safe environment and see possible outcomes of their actions. It also enables you to see where weaknesses and vulnerabilities may exist. Scenarios progress in stages and each stage can be evaluated for progress and problems before proceeding to the next stage.[56]

An underutilized technique that can be combined with scenario modeling is the Delphi technique. The Delphi technique elicits information from a variety of experts concerning an aspect of a disaster.[57] The experts are not allowed to communicate with each other and are given a specified time to respond.[58] This technique utilizes expert knowledge for planning and problem solving. "Successive questionnaires will become progressively more focused on the key issues and will elicit more and more detail."[59] This can be especially useful if you work with security and law enforcement personnel.

Lectures

The most common form of training is that of lectures, often augmented with audio-visual aids. This can be the least expensive to conduct. However, it can be difficult to engage learners and ensure that the information is retained.

Training Topics

Training courses should cover established policies and procedures. Training on policies and procedures should be on a need-to-know basis and be specific to the job. Other training topics should include any update to laws and regulations, crime prevention techniques, identifying suspicious behaviors, incident management, crisis response, recognizing the sounds of gunshots, and security awareness. Security topics such as identifying suspicious behaviors and crime prevention techniques can be provided to all staff. All staff and volunteers also need to be trained on how to report incidents, who to report them to, and how else to respond.

Evaluating the Effectiveness of a Training Program

It is important to assure that information is not only learned, but retained so that it can be used in an emergency. This can be accomplished through periodic drills similar to fire drills, short quizzes, and questionnaires.

Updating Training Programs

Training programs, just like policies and procedures, should be evaluated on a regular basis such as annually. They should also be updated when any of the following occur:

1. After an event either at the religious institution itself or in the surrounding community
2. After a change in law, regulations, policy, procedure, or equipment
3. When new staff or volunteers are hired

Final Thoughts

Accurate and informative training, combined with periodic evaluation and refresher training is vital to security. The courses do not have to be fancy or given by professional trainers. However, they must be accurate, relevant, and consistent. They should provide trainees with the opportunity to ask questions and receive clarification.

The next chapters focus on special considerations for religious institutions. Chapter 16 concerns executive protection of religious leaders. Chapter 17 helps assess the need for less lethal weapons and firearms. Chapter 18 concerns finding resources within your membership and the community to establish security partnerships. Chapter 19 focuses on special considerations for the most vulnerable population at your facility—children and youth.

End Notes

1. Crowe T. D., and Fennelly L. J., *Crime Prevention through Environmental Design*, Third Edition (Boston: Butterworth-Heinemann, 2013).
2. Ibid.
3. McGlown K. J., *Terrorism and Disaster Management: Preparing Healthcare Leaders for the New Reality* (Chicago: Health Administration Press, 2004).

4. Ibid.
5. Ibid.
6. Alexander D., *Principles of Emergency Planning and Management* (New York: Oxford University Press, 2002).
7. Ibid.
8. Ibid.
9. Ibid.
10. Ibid.
11. Ibid.
12. Ibid.
13. Ibid.
14. Maiden R. P., Paul R., and Thompson C., eds., *Workplace Disaster, Preparedness, Response, and Management* (Haworth Press, 2006).
15. See note 6 above.
16. See note 14 above, p. 81.
17. See note 6 above.
18. See note 3 above.
19. See note 6 above.
20. See note 6 above.
21. See note 6 above.
22. See note 6 above.
23. See note 6 above.
24. See note 6 above.
25. See note 6 above.
26. See note 6 above.
27. See note 6 above.
28. See note 6 above.
29. See note 6 above.
30. See note 6 above.
31. See note 6 above, p. 291.
32. See note 6 above.
33. See note 6 above.
34. See note 6 above.
35. See note 6 above.
36. See note 6 above.
37. See note 6 above.
38. See note 6 above.
39. See note 6 above.
40. See note 6 above.
41. See note 6 above.
42. Kizakevich P. N. et al., *Chemical Casualty Simulation for Emergency Preparedness Training*, 2003. Retrieved from http://www.rvht.info/pubs%5Ciitsec_chem.12.02.03.pdf.
43. See note 3 above.
44. See note 3 above.
45. See note 3 above.
46. See note 3 above.
47. See note 3 above.
48. See note 3 above.
49. See note 3 above, p. 68.

50. Haddow G. D., Bullock J. A., and Coppola D. P., *Introduction to Emergency Management*, Fourth Edition (Boston: Butterworth-Heinemann, 2011).

51. Ibid, p. 167.

52. See note 6 above.

53. See note 6 above.

54. See note 6 above.

55. See note 6 above.

56. See note 6 above.

57. See note 6 above.

58. See note 6 above.

59. See note 6 above, p. 51.

Keeping the Principal Safe

16

The principal of a religious institution, and often their family, can become a target for various reasons. As a result, your organization should consider hiring protection for them.

There are a multitude of reasons why the principal or other religious leaders may become a target of violence.

1. Controversial statements
2. Political stances
3. Media exposure
4. Disgruntled or disillusioned employees/attendees
5. Workplace violence

Religious leaders who make public stances on controversial or political issues such as gay marriage, the role of women, abortion, birth control, euthanasia, gun control, and others may become targets for either supporting or not supporting a particular stance. Support for a particular political party or candidate can trigger a dangerous response in some individuals.

When a person is on television, they attract people who want some of that fame and success. To some individuals, a way to gain notoriety is to assault the famous person. They may stalk the individual and threaten their family. In addition, the increased presence of many religious institutions on the internet and social media can invite negative attention as well.

Disgruntled or disillusioned people may have a grudge against a particular leader. Perhaps the leader has been counseling a couple and one party believes that leader is trying to split them up. They may blame the failure of their marriage on the "interference" of the religious institution. This is also true in domestic violence situations.

Other people who have been counseled or who are relatives of someone whose counseling was unsuccessful may take their anger and frustration out on the leader of the institution they blame for their troubles.

People that have been excommunicated from their church could possibly become a threat. Anyone with a personal grievance could potentially become an adversary.

Location of the religious institution is another vulnerability. In inner cities, the possibility of violence through gang retaliation has been a high concern. Its proximity to high-crime areas may also bring unwanted attention.

Deciding If You Need Executive Protection

If your religious organization decides protection for the principal and their family is necessary, they should hire professionals. This task is too important and possibly too dangerous for amateurs.

Many states regulate these professionals variously known as personal protection specialists, executive protection, etc. State regulations dictate that individuals are properly licensed and trained as well as having passed a background check. However, this should not prevent you from practicing due diligence and verifying training, licensing, and a clean background check.

Executive protection can evolve from the basics to highly advanced methods and equipment. Determining what you need is the dilemma. Creating a threat assessment will allow you to collect data and make a decision from that information. There are different levels of threats from death and bodily injury to verbal slander. All need to be handled in their own way.

The two main elements of personal protection are "harm" and "embarrassment." Harm is the most severe and important because of the possibility of assassination, assault, and kidnapping. Embarrassment, although, can be quite damaging to one's image as mentioned in Chapter 13 concerning intangible capital. However, reputation can be recovered easier than losing a life.

Threat Identification

Threat identification is a key element in this whole process as mentioned in Chapter 4 on evaluating risk. Not knowing what or who you are protecting yourself against is a burden and unproductive. Once the threat is identified, it must be described in specific terms to help determine the principal's vulnerabilities and to establish a protection plan. Identifying the threat is very important because you can focus on protecting against that specific threat. You are in a far worse position when you cannot identify the threat.

24-Hour Protection

24-hour protection can have multiple meanings to multiple people: Some might work in their home; others might work out their back door; and some might work in multiple cities, states, or countries. Whatever the situation is, there is a solution.

Before a threat has been identified, the principal should be proactive in their own security. Situational awareness most of the time can deter something from happening. Recognition of a threat or accident can prevent you from having a bad day. Keeping your head on a swivel is a popular term in the security field. This means that you probably should not be texting and worrying about what is on your phone or tablet while you are walking, running, driving, swimming, working, etc. Keeping your head up and noticing what is going on around you might prevent you from even being targeted. Applying this simple technique with your family could prevent one of you from being kidnapped or hurt.

Situational awareness is a good place to start with noticing what is going on around you. But knowing what to look for might be hard if you do not have the knowledge to recognize the signs. All around the country, hands-on personal safety classes are being offered at private schools and online. Reach out to these resources and collect as much information on protecting yourself as possible. You might have not signed up to be a person of interest, but during your path someone might make you one because of your profession. Staying proactive in protecting yourself and your family is in your best interest.

Once you learn more and apply these new techniques and principles in your everyday life, it will become second nature. You will start taking different streets to work, walking with your head on a swivel, and looking for signs of security threats. These new habits will filter down through your family. Having open discussions on security is a good way to get their mind kick-started.

Having the resources to hire personal protection specialists is not an option for everyone. However, if it is, it is highly recommended. Throughout each section, we will talk about what to do if it is not an option, then we will talk about if personal protection is an option.

Residential Protection

Protection at the residence can be an interesting topic. Do you want it to look like and be a hard target or be a hard target without looking like one? You might not want your home to look like a bunker, or on the other hand, you might be okay with it. Maybe you are not dealing with a single family home; but instead you are trying to protect a condo, townhouse, high-rise building, or even a ranch with hundreds or thousands of acres. You are going to have to adapt to the situation.

If you decide that the residence needs more protection than the locks on the doors and windows, you have a couple of options. After completing your threat assessment and determining what the level of protection is, it would be recommended to go one level higher than what is needed. This process is called making a hard target. The hard target is something that deters threats as you want to make the threat feel that there is no chance for success. The harder the target, the less chance a threat has for success.

It is important to have responses to different threats. No matter where you live, these responses can be practiced with drills. Fire drills are a good place to start because everyone has participated in one. From elementary school all the way to corporate jobs, people have been practicing fire drills. Having a meeting place set outside is a key to this plan. Once everyone knows where they are meeting, then you can go over exits to get there. Depending on the residence, everyone's exit might not be the same. It is important to practice these exits so everyone is familiar with them. Having fire alarms, fire extinguishers, and even sprinklers are three things to prevent further catastrophe.

Once you have completed the fire drills, you can move to different scenarios. Home invasion, arson, natural disasters, power outages—all of these would have a reactionary plan. Incorporating these into the protection plan is something that, once developed and drilled, would just need to be talked about and drilled a couple times a year.

Cameras have been around forever, however, in recent years, they have been affordable for the homeowner. Setting up a camera system is something that anyone can do. If you want a direct connection system or even a wireless system, they are available. This is a simple and inexpensive threat deterrent to install and can be connected directly to your computer or phone wherever you are located. To take every precaution and use it to its full capabilities would be recommended. You can check the house for threats before you ever get home and put yourself in a bad situation. You can have eyes outside without stepping a foot outside and putting yourself in harm's way.

Using cameras to your advantage is broadening your situational awareness to another level. Having the resources to relieve the sense of vulnerability is a confidence that one needs to stay proactive against attack. These are all things that you yourself can do to make yourself a hard target. However, when the threat is so great that it outweighs your own deterrents, then it might be time to look to the professionals.

Even though you have used and taken advantage of the resources that were available, there is always another level of protection. Coming from the personal protection point of view, the residence can be a point of weakness.

Ideally the protection detail would love to put you in a concrete bunker underground and not let you out until the threat has been neutralized. However, that is just not possible since you are going to have to able to make services and meetings and carry on with your everyday activities.

The probability of the home being designed with security and protection in mind is highly unlikely. Also, the location might be a problem. It would be recommended that the location of the residence be closer to the facility rather than farther away. This allows the protection detail to run more efficiently.

Since you have been proactive in learning security practices, you are going to be able to have a more educated conversation with the protective detail. Having a principal that is aware of the security risks and understands why the detail wants to do certain things is a dream come true. Being able to trust the detail and have confidence in what they can do relieves that sense of vulnerability we talked about earlier.

Facility Protection

Like the residence, if you decide that the facility needs more protection than the locks on the doors and windows, the same principles apply. Cameras, lighting, alarms, and even fencing are options protecting the facility. However, this brings us back to the appearance of protection. Do you want the facility to look like a bunker or not?

You have a couple of options. After completing your threat assessment and determining what the level of protection is, it is recommended to go one level higher than what is needed. This process is called making a hard target. The hard target is something that deters threats by thinking that it is a harder possibility for success. The harder the target, the less chance a threat has for success.

The basics of making a facility a hard target would be to install decoy cameras and signs of video surveillance, e.g., security signs and outside lighting. A more advanced method would be to make those things real. Cameras that work with CCTV monitoring, either from a control room or from a mobile network, could be monitored by multiple people. Upgrading the alarm system with one that has a physical response would be a great addition.

The decision to tell the members of the religious institution will be a hard one. Do you hide the fact that there has been a threat no matter what level? Do you tell everyone so they can take the proper precautions for the safety of their family? Do you tell just certain members for security purposes? These are the types of questions you are going to have to answer. Because a threat has been made against you, it does not mean that someone else could not get injured or killed during an attempt on your life.

If and when you decide to tell everyone, the drills should start as soon as possible and not just fire drills either. Now that we are going to have more people, the drills need to be broader. The first ones that should be considered after the basic ones are active shooter drills. What is everyone going to do if shots are fired in the facility?

Active shooter drills are becoming more popular with the rise of active shooter attempts. These drills can and will saves lives if and when an attempt happens. Again, being proactive on learning about protecting your facility is highly beneficial. Bringing in professionals for seminars or classes will raise awareness in the institution. There are a lot of different methods to respond or react to an active shooter situation, from barricading yourself in a room to finding the quickest way out of the facility to finding safety and calling emergency services.

If you have the option to bring in a protective detail, they will have plans for every contingency and execute drills so you have the highest survivability rate. Depending on the level of security, it can be a small detail for just protecting the principal or a larger one to have eyes on everyone in the facility.

Protection When You Travel

Whether or not the threat has been identified is what makes traveling easier or that much harder. When you have identified the threat, you can plan your travels accordingly. Determining where the threat is located and what resources they have can determine where or how you travel.

If the threat is local and does not have the resources to travel and you have the proper channels to keep an eye on them, it would make your travel plans a lot easier. If the threat is in a certain part of the country or world, then you would have to take precautions when visiting those locations. Information is the most important aspect of protecting yourself, not just in your home but everywhere. If you can determine what the threat is doing, you can make the necessary plans to stay away from them.

However, if you do not have that information, it will drastically change how you travel, how you protect yourself, and you will never develop that sense of security. Protecting yourself against something that may be real or potentially fake while you are traveling is never a good situation to be in. Change the way you travel—from flying when you would usually drive or drive when you would normally fly. Habits are what give the threat a way to plan and carry out an attack.

Changing those habits continuously so the threat can never develop a pattern is what you are trying to do.

Changing the route you take every day or every time you visit a certain location is something you should be proactively doing anyway. Travel discretely and do not let people know what your schedule is, except the ones that need to know. Publicly advertising your schedule is not a good idea when trying to deter a threat.

But, if the threat is high enough that you feel these options are not enough, then it is time to make a decision to hire a protective detail. If the resources allow it, then it is highly recommended. This would make the likelihood of an attack drop significantly.

Just having a team planning your travels and holding current information on where you are traveling in advance, as well as having multiple people on the ground, is a huge advantage. This would also relieve you of having to plan and coordinate when you have other things to get done and worry about.

Protection for Your Family

We have talked a little on family involvement in this chapter and will continue it here. Having your family involved is very important. The one thing that could be used against you is your family, and it is important that they are safe and secure. Having them work on their situational awareness is important to their safety. They might recognize something that was overlooked, or maybe they are being used to get close to you. These things need to be considered and are why they should be involved in developing security practices.

When threats feel that they cannot get to their primary target, they will look for other ways to hurt the principal. Kidnapping is one of the most effective ways to hurt the principal. Having your family recognize these dangers is important. Now, you assume the protective detail role and want to lock them in a bunker until the threat is neutralized. If the threat is considered that high and the resources are available, then you would get a protective detail for your family.

Personal Protection Detail

Additionally, we are adding some of the positions that are in a protective detail or team. Shift leader (SL) or team leaders (TL) have responsibility for the whole team and principal. Personal security officers (PSO), another name for a bodyguard (B), are usually with the principal 24/7. Right rear (RR) is responsible for covering the right and rear side of the formation you are in. Left rear (LR) is responsible for covering the left and rear side of the formation. There could also be right front (RF), left front (LF), and advance (Adv), which would be a point man.

These are just some of the positions that could make up a protection detail. Lay out some of the positions and what their responsibilities would be. Depending on the size of the detail, there could be anywhere from one person to 20 in the personnel security detail. Advance teams make sure the event or facility is safe before the principal even arrives. The team could be as small as one person with the principal when discretion is necessary.

Assessing the Need for Less Lethal Tools and Firearms

17

Arming members of the security staff or allowing attendees to be armed is not a decision to be made lightly. There are many factors to be considered when deciding to allow armed individuals in your facility.

1. Training
2. Continuous training
3. Use of force continuum
4. Budget
5. Close quarters considerations
6. What type of less lethal
7. What type of firearm
8. Liability

Use of Force Continuum

Before we can discuss choosing which weapons security team members or private security professionals utilize, we must look at the use of force continuum. The use of force continuum is a set standard that should be in every program.

This standard that has worked for police officers and private security professional for years can also work for you. It can be compared to the rules of engagement the military uses. The reason the continuum is successful is it allows everyone to be on the same page—the same sheet of music. Without it, everyone would respond differently to the situation.

The use of force continuum is also a training aid to introduce into new scenarios. Have scenarios that physical presence and verbal commands contain the situation. But, also have scenarios that escalate the use of force.

What this scenario base training does is it allows the trainees to get the proper mental conditioning. The proper mental conditioning prepares the mind for if or when the time comes that you are going to have to raise the level of force. The levels raise from physical presence, verbal commands, hands only control, and less lethal control to deadly force as shown in (Figure 17.1).

By doing these scenario base drills, you are also improving your judgment. By improving your decision-making and judgment, you will make quicker decisions when you need to, escalating the amount of force necessary or deescalating the amount of force. The objective is to use the least amount of force necessary to control the subject.

Remember, there is no set-in-stone standard to write a use of force continuum. There are plenty of examples out there, and you can probably get help through your

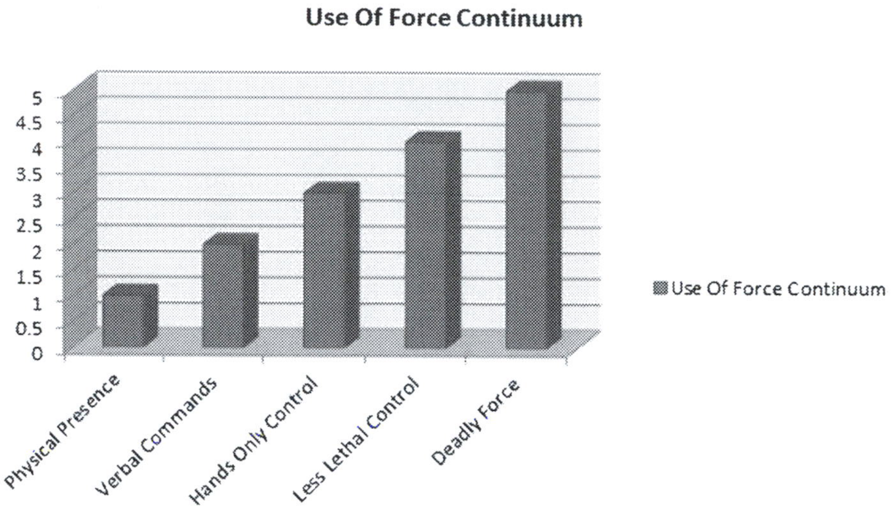

Use Of Force Continuum

Figure 17.1 The use of force continuum.

local law enforcement agency or private security professional. Do your due diligence for the protection of the institution against liability or legal issues.

Training

Training is something that we are going to talk about a lot in this section. Training is sometimes underrated, and that is the last thing it should be. Here is an example. Anyone can make a phone call, show up to the class, go through the motions, and pass whatever test there is. That person will walk away with a certificate that says, for example, "Certified in Baton." That person then will think that the training is over and never practice with the baton again.

The problem with this is they are completely wrong. The next time that person deploys their baton without practicing is when things go wrong. Complacency is one of the biggest anchors when it comes to training. If and when you decide to implement less lethal or lethal weapons into your program, do not fall into this type of mind-set.

Setting up weekly, monthly, bi-annual, and even an annual training program is a place to start. Weekly training would be the best for not losing the skill it takes to be proficient in using any type of tool or weapon. However, the time to coordinate this with volunteers that have families, careers, and other important things going on is hard to obtain. Monthly training is optimal; with this time frame, you can schedule things weeks out, so they can plan to be there. It is plenty of time in between training sessions to keep morale high and plan new and interesting training sessions.

Bi-annual training fits in with programs that just cannot have weekly or monthly training sessions. If the first two just cannot happen, the bi-annual type is the one for you. Bi-annual training is great for programs on a strict time restriction. Twice a year you ask everyone to come in and train either on what they are already certified in or something new. You can bring in guest speakers or instructors to update credentials or teach new techniques.

Last, there is annual training. It is certainly not at the top of the list, but it is better than not training at all. Annual training is for those who just do not have the budget or resources to handle a more productive training program. This is the risk that you take with annual training. Yes, you are training; and yes, it is better than no training. However, it is not recommended.

Let us finish with an example about why training is so important. I am going to give you some clues on something all of us train to do; see if you can guess what it is. For most of us, this is something you wanted to do your whole young life. If you live in a big city, this is something you complain about every day. For some of us, once you do it for many years, you do not want to do it that much anymore. Last, this is something that at one time or another you said, "Some people are not good at that." Did you get it?

Driving is something that most of us train on daily. Now, some of us have been driving for years, and still, some of us are not that good at it. Imagine you are riding with a new driver or someone who does not train to drive daily. How does it make you feel when this happens? You just want to get out as fast as you can. Now, picture that same person with a less lethal tool or lethal weapon. Now, hopefully, you have put it together. Just because you have a license to do something does not make you proficient or safe to use that tool.

Budget

Now, we can talk about the perfect training program and so forth. But, you have to mold or create your program around what you can afford. We are going to talk about the options you have to choose from. Batons, Tasers, stun guns, OC spray, and, finally, firearms are all potential items you are going to look at. Included will be the comparison of price, maintenance, training, durability, and liability.

One last thing to consider is to allow members that are armed professionals (i.e., sworn police officers) already attending the institution to carry during the services. Members who also have a career in private security or military could be used in these situations. Some might already have the training that you are looking for and may even be certified to teach others.

Less Lethal Tools/Weapons

When the physical presence has not been enough to contain the situations, it is time to implement less lethal tools into the program. Less lethal tools are carried to raise the level of force necessary to overcome the adversary. When less lethal tools are carried, it is not to have deadly force. Without proper and continuous training, deadly force can and will happen.

Just like hardening a target that we talked about in the last chapter, you are basically doing that to your security staff. If you decide to open carry these tools so they are visible to the attendees, you are letting everyone know that if something happens, you are going to protect and defend them. You are also saying that if someone is going to get out of line, they will be on the receiving end of one of these tools. Most of the time, people do not want to be on the receiving end of any less lethal or, more importantly, a lethal weapon. This, in turn, will hopefully prevent anything from happening.

If the decision to conceal these tools is made, then make an announcement that less lethal tools have been implemented in the program. This will let people know that they are on the premises and not to panic if someone sees one in an open jacket or coat.

Baton

Batons are a great choice for a less lethal tool. They are fairly inexpensive and easy to maintain. The initial training and certification can usually be done locally, which is convenient if you are on a small budget. Some of the pros of batons are their light weight, their ability to be concealed, durability, and effectiveness. A person can deploy a baton and control a subject when properly trained. Baton maintenance is almost nonexistent. Keep it clean, apply some rust protection, and it takes care of the rest. If something does break, it will be inexpensive to replace the part.

Cons of the baton are when a person is not proficient in using the baton, it can be taken from them and used against them. Liability with everything is a risk. Hitting a subject in the wrong place can be quite damaging and even lethal. That is why it is extremely important to train with it.

When choosing the baton, you also have to consider close quarters. For example, having a 6-ft-tall person with a 2 to 3-ft baton who is deployed in a hallway that is 2.5 to 6-ft wide with a ceiling that is as low as 7 ft in some places might not be a good idea. These are the things that you need to think about when choosing the tools for your program. Is the baton something we want to introduce to the program? Where are we going to be carrying the baton? Can we afford the baton?

Tasers

Now Tasers are great and very effective. But for some reason, people do not like things pointing at them that can really hurt them. For good reason, I might add. Nobody wants to get hit with a Taser. For example, the online video where the 2000-pound bull gets hit with a Taser and it drops to the ground should be shown to everyone. When people watch this video, the last thing they want is to get hit with a Taser.

So, all of these examples make Tasers great additions to your security program. So, with greater reward comes greater cost. The initial training and certification can also be done locally. Some pros of the Taser are its light weight, it is somewhat concealable, durable, and highly effective. Someone could draw the Taser and usually control the subject with verbal commands from that point. However, you are going have some instances when verbal commands are not going to work.

Maintenance is fairly simple. Check to make sure there is no damage to the gun, the cartridge, or the replacement cartridges. You can purchase training cartridges to check and make sure it works properly.

One of the biggest cons of the Taser is you have to reload it when or if you miss your target. You are going to have to decide how and what you are going to carry with it. Are you going to carry an extra cartridge as recommended? Now this brings up a training issue. Not training with what you carry like we talked about earlier is going to be a factor.

Close quarters is going to be a factor with this as well. If you have other people near you, you are going to have to think about one of your safety rules. Know your target and what is beyond it.

Finally, you have to think about the liability of deploying and actually firing the Taser. The repercussion of firing and not hitting the target and potentially hitting an innocent person is going to bring legal issues.

Oleoresin Capsaicin (OC) Spray

OC spray is another less lethal tool to have in your program. Having been hit with OC, I can confirm it is not a good thing. Nobody wants to get sprayed, misted, or foamed with OC. Picking which method of deployment is up to you. The cost is not that expensive, but there is a shelf life. So, you will have to keep a record of the dates and replace them accordingly. You should be able to find initial training and certification locally.

Maintenance is pretty easy. Make sure that it stays clean and protected so it does not get punctured. The record keeping of the expiration date falls into this category as well. The pros of OC are it is fairly easy to deploy and carry. It is concealable, light weight, and durable in most cases. It disorientates the subject most of the time to where they comply with verbal commands.

OC does have some cons. It does disorient, but someone can still function after getting sprayed with OC. You do not have to have your eyes open to punch, kick, or counterattack. You also have to be pretty close to someone to accurately hit them. This will put you in someone's reactionary gap where they might be able to move closer. So, when they move, you might not spray them where you would want to.

Close quarters is very important with OC and how you deploy it. In a room or hallway, it can not only affect the person sprayed but also the people around them. The person deploying it, their partner, or anyone else close to the situation could get exposed to OC. So, in that case, foam might be something to consider.

Like all of these, liability comes into play here. Deploying OC and having something happen to innocent people around could affect them. Someone getting sprayed with OC and getting serious respiratory issues is a concern. These are all things to think about when choosing what is right for your program.

Firearms

There are many things we could talk about with firearms. Really, so much, it could be a book of its own. We are going to try and break each topic down just enough to give you the basic information. We will talk about price, maintenance, pros, cons, training, close quarters, and liability. You are going to have to your due diligence in this section as well. Make sure there are no legal issues. You might have to get certified through the state to have a security program or run the security detail background to make sure there are no discrepancies.

The initial cost per person is going to be at least 10 times more compared to less lethal. The cost will be even more if you carry both. Training, firearms, carry ammo, practice ammo, holsters, belts, jackets, extra magazines, magazine pouches, handcuffs, handcuff pouches, OC, OC pouch, flashlight, flashlight holster, Taser, Taser holster, extra cartridges, baton, baton holster, soft armor, hard armor, and much more—these are just examples of what you are going to choose from.

The initial cost will be higher plus the long-term cost of certain things like ammo and maintenance. I am not trying to scare anyone into not implementing firearms. In fact, that is the last thing I want to do. I just want you to understand some of the costs. You are going to have to consider the long-term resources needed to support a security program.

Firearms are very intimidating to some people and a great visual deterrent. If you plan on concealing them, again someone should make an announcement that they are present. Training with firearms is very important, and the complacency that we talked about earlier is the last you want to do with firearms training. The bullet that comes out of the gun does not stop until it hits something. So, liability is something to think about when dealing with close quarters, poor training, and safety.

Pistols

Pistols are the most popular firearm for security work. They are very convenient to work with and very easy to carry concealed. If you decide not to have security conceal, there are plenty of belt and holster options to choose from. The pros of pistols are that they are very convenient, light weight compared to long guns, include plenty of options, ammo capacity, and available training. There are plenty more but this just gives you an idea.

Maintenance is pretty straight forward. Every new gun comes with an owner's manual that shows you how and what to maintain on your firearm. Follow the directions, and you should be fine. If you would like to know how to break the firearms completely down, there are armorer's courses available that will show you how.

There are many options to choose from when seeking out training with a pistol. One recommendation would be to check the instructors that are teaching the class. Make sure they have the skills to teach you what you need to know. It would not be a problem to have a meeting with the instructors to see if they will be a good fit. Teaching style, personality, and knowledge of the topic would be some things that you would be looking for during this meeting. This will apply with all the training you look for.

Rifles and Shotguns

Rifles and shotguns are a great addition to your security program. The long-range capabilities are far superior to a pistol. Rifles offer more round capacity and a higher rate of fire. Shotguns are great for close quarters and breaching. You can control how the shotgun fires with chokes and choosing different types of ammo for different situations. Both would bring another level security to your program.

You would have the same options with maintenance that you have with the pistol. Also, like pistol training, you would want to look for the best training options you have available. It also would be good to send out a couple people from the team to instructor schools. Then, you could start training in house. It would keep the overall cost down from sending everyone.

Concealed Carry Laws

Concealed carry laws can be different in every state. The best way to find out what your state allows is to look at the state's official Website. Here, you will find everything you need. If you cannot find what you need, a call to the state police will be able to point you in the right direction. If you decide to carry concealed firearms in your security program, please make sure you comply with the law. Carrying concealed may have less of a deterrent effect on adversaries, but may make staff and attendees more comfortable. You will have to take this into account when deciding on allowing concealed weapons.

Considerations

Regardless of the type of weapon used, there are some basic considerations:

1. Written policies
   a. Use of force
   b. Requirements for carrying weapons
      - Training
      - Background checks
2. Training
   a. Proper deployment
   b. Safety
   c. Accuracy
   d. Close quarters considerations
   e. Liability
3. Communication
   a. In case of an incident, local law enforcement should be aware that there are those at the facility who are authorized to carry and use weapons.

Final Thoughts

Even if you decide not to allow individuals in your facility to carry weapons, you still need a use of force policy. Individuals can be seriously injured or killed from physical assaults with or without objects. You need to establish how people should respond to being attacked or having an object thrown at them. Regardless of the type of weapons chosen, anyone who has access to them must be properly trained. Remember the use of force continuum. If the only weapon provided is a gun, that is what will be used. Less lethal weapons provide other options to use instead.

Establishing Security Partnerships 18

One of the most effective methods for securing a facility is to establish security partnerships. There are several partnerships you can form that work toward improving the overall security of your facility. Partnerships provide support, resources, and expertise that can help you in all stages of incident management from planning to response and recovery.

Partnerships can be formal or informal. Formal partnerships require a contract for services and are legally binding, which may transfer some liability from your facility to the partner. Contracting with a private security firm for services is an example of a formal partnership.

Informal partnerships are not legally binding and, therefore, do not provide liability protections. Still, informal partnerships can provide valuable resources. The majority of your partnerships will likely be informal.

Benefits of Partnerships

1. Expertise
2. Support
3. Resources
4. Shared liability
5. Help build and sustain public support for the religious institution[1]

Within the Organization

The majority of your partnerships will likely come from within the religious institution. Do not underestimate the resources you have in your staff, employees, members, and attendees. You may have security, emergency services, or law enforcement personnel using your facility.

Most religious institutions are already familiar with using volunteers to provide various activities and perform various services. There are a number of roles members can assume to aid in the security of the religious institution. These include the following:

1. Protection committee
2. Security teams
3. Threat assessment committee

Protection Committee

First, you should establish a formal protection committee, consisting of both members and facility managers, who will have comprehensive oversight concerning the activities, policies, and procedures designed to ensure the safety and security of the facility, its employees, and members.[2] The committee size is dependent upon the size of the congregation, and membership should reflect the demographics of the congregation itself.[3] The committee performs many tasks within the sphere of security for its religious institution.

Serving as a direct liaison with local law enforcement, it may also be responsible for developing the security plan and conducting a security risk assessment or at least contacting professionals to consult on design and implementation. The committee should review policies and procedures and create a guidebook of facility security policies and procedures.

Additional tasks may include, but are not limited to, interacting with risk management representatives and inventorying equipment and other items of value. It can also assist in comprehensive physical security and oversee the use of security officers for traffic control or special events.

Security Teams

Security teams are typically comprised of members who volunteer to perform certain functions for the organization. This can include monitoring parking lots, handling money, or serving as ushers or greeters. Security teams do not have to consist of professional security personnel unless weapons are involved. However, they must be well-trained, discrete, alert, aware of their surroundings, and attentive to detail. They should maintain a friendly and welcoming demeanor while introducing themselves to strangers.[4]

To be effective, it is vital that all employees and volunteers are trained in their roles and that established policy and procedures are adhered to each and every time. They should be trained to recognize suspicious behavior as well as how to handle potential violators. They should work out some type of signaling system to alert each other to potential problems without letting the suspect know they are being watched. In addition, they should have cell phones preset to dial 911 immediately in case of an emergency.[5]

Security team members take turns watching the parking lot, facilities, restrooms, and offices particularly during services.[6] They "patrol" the grounds to serve as a deterrent to inappropriate behavior, to report suspicious behavior, and to respond to emergencies. Religious institutions can also request that members drive by the facility and through the parking lots periodically. However, they are not to confront potential strangers. Encourage members to be alert for unusual or suspicious activities and contact the police if they believe something is out of the ordinary.

Security team members can have the following designations:

1. Greeters/welcoming committee
2. Up front participants

3. Ushers
4. Parking lot attendants

Greeters/Welcoming Committees

Welcoming committees are positioned at key entryways greeting visitors and members. This assures personal contact with everyone who walks into the facility and sends the subliminal message to criminals that they were seen, greeted, and can be identified.[7] They are not to bar anyone from entering the facility unless there is sufficient cause. However, they may quietly ask ushers or other individuals to discretely keep an eye on them.

Up Front Participants

"Up front participants" are security volunteers who sit in the front of the building and look out over the audience.[8] They are in a key position to observe the entranceway as well as those sitting in the pews. Additional volunteers can be seated throughout the facility and in balconies or alcoves to watch for suspicious behavior. There should also be those trained in security stationed by doors, alarms, phones, etc.[9]

Ushers

While ushers often have other tasks to perform during services, they can still serve as security by keeping an eye on attendees, escorting individuals to their seats, and maintaining custody of monetary offerings. During services, they should be stationed at various observation points so they can observe attendees.

Parking Lot Attendants

These individuals ensure that traffic in and out of the parking lot flows smoothly. They can funnel pedestrian traffic into "choke points" where individuals are met by the welcoming committee. This prevents individuals from entering unannounced and ensures that everyone is seen so they can possibly be identified later if need be.

Also known as "umbrella patrols," they can take umbrellas out to attendees and escort them inside during bad weather.[10] This is not only courteous, but it provides an opportunity to again make sure they know who is entering the building as well as make a brief survey of the parking lot to ensure everything is secure.

Threat Assessment Committee

A threat assessment committee's function is to investigate reported instances of threatening behavior, to determine the seriousness of the threat (i.e., the likelihood of acting on that threat) and to plan an appropriate response.

In addition, they serve as a specific place for others to submit information discreetly that will be taken seriously. They also may work with potential offenders by referring them confidentially to mental health programs and various social services as necessary.

The threat assessment committee should include leaders of the religious institution, security staff, and other members who have some expertise in the area. At some stage in the threat assessment process, local police, mental health professionals, and representatives of pertinent social service agencies may become involved.

Threat Assessment Committee Goals[11]

1. Take all threats seriously.
2. Treat every contact with respect and discretion.
3. Document.
4. Evaluate complainant's motivation.
5. Determine needed intervention.
6. Present complaint to all members of the team.
7. Bring in additional experts as needed.
8. Take appropriate action.
9. Implement security measures.
10. Respond to media queries.
11. Conduct follow-up.

These groups fit nicely in with the general mission of the religious institution as they seek to welcome those who are sincere into the congregation and ensure the safety and security of the church as a whole. They are effective in that "the greatest threat to a criminal is being identified."[12] Therefore, they will strive to remain anonymous, which is difficult to do when there are so many people around who are interested.

Outside the Organization

There are a wide variety of community resources at the local, state, and national levels that can provide assistance before, after, and during a crisis.

Private Security

Private security professionals provide a range of services such as consulting, conducting risk assessments and physical security surveys, installing security devices and equipment, training, monitoring, and response. They can be hired for a specific job such as installing a CCTV or alarm system, or they can be hired for consulting on security plan design. These formal partnerships should involve a contract specifying the scope of services that will be provided.

Some states regulate security personnel or the businesses they work for, setting minimum standards for training, experience, and background checks. In those states, it is illegal to work with individuals or businesses that are not properly and currently licensed. You can check with your state's private security regulatory agency in order to find out if a business or individual is legally allowed to perform security services. However, not all states regulate private security personnel or businesses, so it is important to research any company with whom you wish to conduct business.

Steps for Choosing a Security Company

1. Research companies through the Better Business Bureau.
2. Check licensing standards for your state and ensure the company and individuals are properly and currently licensed, registered, or certified.
3. Check references
4. Compare services and prices.
5. Set up demonstrations.

Establishing partnerships with local security companies can improve security for your facility. In fact, some companies may be willing to conduct a training course or perform a risk assessment or physical security survey for free or at a reduced rate.

Industry Associations

There are many private security industry associations that can provide much-needed expertise in security matters. They can provide tips on selecting security services, licensing requirements for services, how to establish a contract, hiring consultants, and many other valuable topics. They can provide resources in the form of books or articles on topics that are of concern to the religious institution. In addition, many provide training courses on particular topics that can be taken by those who are charged with protecting the facility. Many also have developed codes and standards for their respective fields.

If you have questions or concerns, contact the association for advice. They also have lists of members who may be able to provide the expertise needed for a particular concern. Keep in mind, however, that fees are likely to be charged for training, consulting, or other services. You can also contact local chapters of the organizations for assistance.

Below is a partial list of organizations that may be able to provide assistance with your security needs. There are many others. Speak with security professionals that you know to learn about other resources (Figure 18.1).

Public Safety Agencies

While many religious institutions provide counseling and other social services as part of their outreach, there may be those who need care that is beyond the scope of what the religious institution can provide. Establishing partnerships with law enforcement, fire, rescue, emergency services, mental health professionals, and social service agencies can fill in the gaps and ensure that your religious institution is not overwhelmed by the needs of the community.

Law Enforcement

Law enforcement agencies are an invaluable resource. They know the crime rates of the area and what security measures are effective in crime prevention.

Law enforcement is typically reactive. That is, they respond to a situation that has already happened. During an incident, they are responsible for crowd control, communications, distribution of resources, evacuations, and conducting investigations.

Organization	Website	Area of Expertise
ASIS International	www.asisonline.org	Security
National Fire Protection Association	www.nfpa.org	Fire, Building, and Electrical Safety
Associated Locksmiths of America	www.aloa.org	Locks
Electronic Security Association	www.esaweb.org	Electronic Security
Information Systems Security Association	www.issa.org	Information Security
Association of Certified Fraud Examiners	www.acfe.com	Financials Crimes and Fraud
American Crime Prevention Institute	www.acpionline.com	Crime Prevention
National Burglar and Fire Alarm Association	www.alarm.org	Electronic Security

Figure 18.1 Industry Associations.

However, they may be able to perform a security assessment or crime prevention training. Find out what other community policing programs they have and schedule them for your facility.

It is important to establish a rapport with them prior to calling them to respond to an incident. This establishes trust. It also makes response and investigation easier.

Mental Health Professionals

Training courses in recognizing signs of chemical substance abuse, domestic violence, mental illness, depression, and many other topics may be provided to interested members. You may need to refer individuals to these professionals for assistance.

While many religious institutions provide counseling as a service to their members, those with serious issues should be referred to mental health professionals. The National Alliance on Mental Illness (NAMI) has resources specifically designed for religious institutions as part of NAMI FaithNet, which is dedicated to promoting the role of faith in recovery for individuals and families affected by mental illness. NAMI resources can be found at http://www.nami.org/Template.cfm?section=Find_Support.

Fire, Rescue, and Emergency Medical Services

Like law enforcement, these services are typically reactive instead of proactive. However, they also may provide assessments, evaluations, and training to facilities that request assistance. This may include training in fire prevention, first aid, emergency response, and how to establish an emergency shelter. They may also provide guidance on developing emergency operations plans. It also helps if they are familiar with the layout and demographics of the facility prior to an emergency so they can respond quickly and accurately to an emergency.

Federal and State Agencies

Because security often becomes an issue after a natural disaster or a CBRNE event, the preparedness information from state and federal websites can be very useful. Crime and looting can become major issues when buildings are damaged. In addition, charity scams become more prevalent when a major disaster occurs.

As part of their Homeland Security initiatives, the federal government has taken to posting useful information online to aid in preparedness efforts. The information is free to access and can help your planning efforts. While most of the information concerns handling natural disasters, it can still be applicable to security incident response, preparation, mitigation, and recovery efforts.

FEMA offers several free training courses online in disaster management that can aid your facility in planning and preparation for natural disasters as well as active shooter events. These courses can be found at http://training.fema.gov/. Those involved in emergency operations and planning should complete these courses. Additional courses are offered in a classroom setting with the chance to practice new skills and ask questions of professionals.

While the federal websites provide good information, state websites provide information specific to your locality, which provides a more accurate picture of potential threats. Your state's Department of Emergency Management should have tips on its Website concerning potential natural hazards, how to create an emergency response plan, and who to contact for specific emergencies. County Health Department websites also post information regarding health threats.

For a directory of Federal agencies, you can go to http://www.usa.gov/directory/federal/S.shtml. A few are listed in Figure 18.2 with their corresponding area of expertise.

Metropolitan Medical Response System (MMRS)

For a large-scale event in which the religious institution is only one of many victims, some cities and localities have set up a Metropolitan Medical Response System known as MMRS. The MMRS is a unified and integrated approach regarding hospital and public health responses.[13] Its goals are the enhancement of existing response resources to achieve operational capability for a sustained response at the local level for 24 to 48 hours prior to arrival of federal assistance for a chemical, biological, radiological, nuclear, or explosives (CBRNE) event involving 1000 victims or a biological event involving 10,000 victims.[14] Inspired by the 1995 sarin gas attack in Tokyo, the Department of Homeland Security's Domestic Preparedness Program realized that most jurisdictions would be unprepared to handle such an event.[15]

MMRS is an enhancement and integration of existing local capability resources based upon existing first responder/EMS, public health, medical/mental health services, law enforcement, and emergency management systems. Designed to be a

Agency	Website	Area of Expertise
Department of Homeland Security (DHS)	www.dhs.gov	Security, Cybersecurity, and Terrorism
Federal Emergency Management Agency (FEMA)	www.fema.gov	Emergency Preparedness
Federal Bureau of Investigation (FBI)	www.fbi.gov	Scams, Safety, Workplace Violence, Crime Statistics
Bureau of Alcohol, Tobacco, Firearms, and Explosives	www.atf.gov	Arson, Firearms, Explosives
Center for Disease Control and Prevention	www.cdc.gov	Emergency Preparedness for CBRNE emergencies
Department of Health and Human Services	www.hhs.gov www.mentalhealth.gov	Emergency Preparedness, Mental Health Information
Drug Enforcement Administration	www.justice.gov/dea/index.shtml	Drug Abuse and Prevention
Substance Abuse and Mental Health Services Administration	www.samhsa.gov	Suicide Prevention, Mental Health, and Substance Abuse

Figure 18.2 Federal Agencies.

locally organized, trained, and equipped emergency response system, it focuses on individual jurisdictional development to achieve regional capability.[16] Detailed information on the program can be found at http://www.fema.gov/metropolitan-medical-response-system-mmrs-program-archive.

Other Relief Organizations

As you are likely aware, there are a large number of volunteer relief organizations that can aid you in your security efforts, particularly those during the recovery phase. Organizations such as the American Red Cross have expertise in helping individuals deal with trauma. The National Voluntary Organizations Active in Disaster provides resources for victims of various disasters at http://www.nvoad.org/resource-center/.

The American Red Cross and the American Heart Association offer training in first aid, CPR, and use of an AED. Other organizations provide training in helping victims of disasters, serving as an emergency shelter, and incident command just to name a few.

While many relief organizations are focused on recovery from a natural disaster, many of their services are applicable to recovery from a devastating event such as an active shooter situation. Counseling victims, performing first aid, handling the media, coordinating volunteers, and notifying individuals of the status of loved ones are just a few topics that relief organizations have expertise in handling.

Community

Building relationships with the community surrounding your facility is essential, even if you do not provide community outreach services. Many religious institutions work closely with local charities. However, there are other groups within the community that can provide valuable resources.

Residential

If your facility is located in a residential neighborhood, you can have your neighbors report anything suspicious to your security or law enforcement. They can keep an eye on your facility while it is not in use.

Commercial

If your facility is surrounded by commercial businesses, they can provide valuable insight into the types of crimes typically occurring in the area. Look at their physical security features as they are a good indicator of the types of threats they have experienced. Do they have cameras, fences, or alarm systems? Do they have armed or unarmed personnel?

In addition, they may have security cameras that capture part of your facility and/or grounds. It is important to speak with them to find out how their security can affect yours. They may also be willing to share the names and contact information of their security vendors.

Neighborhood Watch

Religious institutions should set up a Neighborhood Watch Program. They can also offer to host local business and neighborhood watches. A mutually beneficial operation, this fosters cooperation and ensures that they will also look out for the facility's interests as well and inform them of any activity that may be detrimental to their organization.

The National Crime Prevention Council offers some tips for organizing a Neighborhood Watch Program.[17]

- Work with local law enforcement as they are critical to the group's credibility and are a valuable source of necessary training and other information.
- Work with victims' services offices to train members in helping victims of crime.
- Hold meetings regularly so members become acquainted with each other and can decide upon program strategies and activities.
- Consider linking with an existing organization—such as a citizens' association, community development office, tenants' association, business association, or housing authority—to provide an existing infrastructure.
- Those who seldom leave their homes can be "window watchers," who look out for children and report any unusual activities.

- Translate materials into any languages needed by non-English speakers in your community and have a translator at meetings, if necessary.
- Gather facts about crime in your neighborhood by checking police reports, conducting victimization surveys, and learning residents' perceptions about crimes as accurate information can reduce the fear of crime.
- Sponsor cleanups of physical conditions and beautification projects as abandoned cars or overgrown vacant lots contribute to crime.
- In a residential area, encourage inhabitants to leave outdoor lights on at night.
- In a commercial area, work with small businesses to repair rundown storefronts, clean up littered streets, and create jobs for young people.
- Emphasize that members are to be alert, observant, and caring and that suspicious activity or crimes should immediately be reported to the police

Other Religious Institutions

Even if they are of different denominations or religious traditions, you can learn valuable information from talking with their leaders. Those who engage in charity scams or affinity frauds often hit multiple religious institutions. Hate crimes are often perpetrated against multiple targets of the same denomination. By discussing your experiences, you can share vital information that will protect other facilities from being swindled.

1. Charity scams
2. Affinity fraud
3. Hate crimes

How to Establish Partnerships

Establishing partnerships starts with deciding what you need and contacting organizations to see what they can provide for you.

1. Decide what you need.
2. Write a policy for developing partnerships.[18]
3. Assign a leader for developing partnerships.[19]
4. Write a leadership action plan for partnerships.[20]
5. Identify a budget with adequate funds.
6. Contact organizations.
7. Find out what they can offer your facility.
8. Welcome them to the facility.
9. Honor their participation.
10. Connect through a focus on security.
11. Set ground rules for involvement.

Standards for Excellent Partnership Programs[21]

1. Teamwork
2. Leadership
3. Plans for action
4. Implementation and facilitation
5. Evaluation
6. Funding
7. Support
8. Network connections

The most important thing to remember is that you are not alone. There is a wealth of resources available, many at no cost, to aid you in protecting your facility. Partnerships must be well planned and carefully executed to be successful.[22] This takes planning, commitment, and time.

End Notes

1. Henderson A. T., Mapp K. L., Johnson V. R. and Davies D., *Beyond the Bake Sale: The Essential Guide to Family-School Partnerships* (New York: The New Press, 2007).
2. Quarles C. L. and Ratliff P. L., *Crime Prevention for Houses of Worship* (Alexandria: American Society for Industrial Security, 2001).
3. Ibid.
4. Aguiar R., *Keeping Your Church Safe* (Maitland: Xulon Press, 2008).
5. See note 2 above.
6. See note 2 above.
7. See note 2 above.
8. See note 2 above.
9. See note 2 above.
10. See note 2 above.
11. .
12. See note 2 above, p. 8.
13. Schwartz J. H., *SPG-CAO UASI Presentation by MMRS Steering Committee Chair Chief James H. Schwartz.* (Transcript of speech given to the MMRS Steering Committee in Fairfax, VA January 2007).
14. See note 13 above.
15. See note 13 above.
16. See note 13 above.
17. http://www.ncpc.org/topics/home-and-neighborhood-safety/neighborhood-watch.
18. Epstein J. L., *School, Family, and Community Partnerships: Your Handbook for Action,* Third Edition (Thousand Oaks: Corwin Press).
19. See note 18 above.
20. See note 18 above.
21. See note 18 above.
22. See note 1 above.

Protecting Children and Youth   19

Most religious institutions provide additional services to their youngest members such as schools, day trips, overnight trips, day care, before and after school care, youth ministries, special events, retreats, and many others. Although the information provided in the previous chapters will protect those who use your facility as a whole, there are special considerations that need to be addressed when dealing with children and youth.

When it comes to keeping children and youth secure, it also means keeping them safe. While other areas of security only tangentially mention safety, it is inextricably linked with security where children and youth are concerned. Security involves protecting the most vulnerable attendees of your facility from harm in all its forms.

There are a number of challenges:[1]

1. Media is quick to place blame without facts.
2. Public opinion is quick to judge incidents and the decisions made by those involved.
3. Lawsuits are frequently the first response.
4. Technology enables misinformation to spread quickly.
5. Even unfounded accusations can have a devastating effect on a facility's reputation.

General Procedures

For every child or youth in your care, you need to have the following:

1. Full name and birth date
2. Emergency contact information
    a. Parents' names
    b. Custodial parental arrangements: Not all biological parents are legally allowed visitation rights. You cannot let the child go with someone just because they know them and are happy to see them.
3. Medical information
    a. Medications
    b. Allergy information: Those with severe allergies can die from contact with even a tiny part of what triggers their allergies. Children with severe allergies should have an EpiPen prescribed specifically for them.
4. For lock-ins or overnight trips:
    a. Injury
    b. Supervision
    c. Youth-to-adult ratios

    d. Safe transportation

    e. Release and authorization-to-treat forms for medical emergencies[1]

Principles of Safety

To maintain safety and security, there are a few general guidelines for all activities involving children and youth. Understanding and applying these principles will prepare staff and volunteers for most incidents.

1. The higher the risk, the greater the supervision required.[2]
2. Read the liability insurance policy for a list of excluded activities.[3]
3. Resist shortcuts. You must be properly prepared for any event or activity.
4. Know the difference between *perceived* danger and *actual* danger.[4]
5. Plan for the worst case scenario.[5]
6. Learn to recognize initial signs of danger.
7. Heed warnings of weather, signage, and law enforcement.
8. Keep in mind any special needs of your group.[6]
9. Train, train, and train some more.
10. Test it first with a simulated run.[7]
11. Make the most of mistakes by learning from them and improving.
12. Take the "my child" test. Would you allow your child to perform the activity?
13. Lead by example. If you do not take safety and security seriously, neither will your staff and/or attendees.
14. Have a plan of action for emergency response.
15. Be alert, aware, and ready for anything.
16. Understand that there is no textbook example. Every event is unique, and what worked once may not work again. Be flexible and adaptable in responding to emergencies.

Abuse and Neglect

One of the most devastating events that can happen to a child or youth is abuse. There are several types of abuse and neglect that you need to protect children and youth from.

1. Sexual abuse
2. Physical abuse
3. Neglect
4. Bullying

    Researchers have reported that sexual predators will gravitate to activities and organizations where fewer protective measures are in place.[8] To protect against this, religious institutions should champion methods for promoting a protective culture that is easily seen and obvious to parent and offender alike.[9]

    It can be difficult to accept that not everyone who is interested in working with children or youth have their best interests at heart. Conversely, it is important to recognize that not all individuals who want to work with them are predators.

Predators fall into two categories: preferential and situational. Preferential molesters seek out situations that allow them to interact with children, whereas situational abusers act on impulse when given an opportunity.[10]

Staff and volunteers should be trained to recognize signs of abuse and neglect. They have an obligation to report suspected abuse to the proper authorities. Check with your state for a legal definition of different types of abuse.[11]

Signs of Abuse

In addition to protecting children and youth from predators within the religious institution including staff and volunteers, those who work with children may be in a unique position to observe signs of abuse, neglect, bullying, and other traumas. Possible signs of different types of abuse and neglect are as follows:

Signs of sexual abuse include depression, promiscuity, sexual diseases, physical ailments, outbursts of anger, and self-abuse.[12] Additional signs include difficulty walking or sitting, bruises or bleeding in the genital area, low self-esteem, and altered sleep patterns or nightmares.[13]

Signs of physical abuse include a consistent pattern of bruises and cuts, burns, facial injuries, self-abuse, anger, and being fearful of adults.[14] Frequent fractures or broken bones, patches of hair loss, and any type of injury to nonmobile infants are other signs of physical abuse.[15]

Signs of neglect include depression, poor hygiene, frequent hunger, and shoplifting or thievery.[16] Emotional abuse signs include depression, suicide attempts, eating disorders, and passive-aggressive behavior.[17]

As with other profiles, it is a pattern of behaviors and signs that you should look for as well as the sheer number of signs displayed. Also, dramatic changes in behavior may indicate that a child or youth is being abused.

A wealth of information can be found at www.childwelfare.gov including recognizing signs of abuse and neglect and how to report suspected abuse to the proper authorities. You can download the fact sheet or get it sent to you for free. They also offer additional resources that can be used to develop your own training programs for staff and volunteers.

Religious leaders who allow a suspected child abuser to work with children can be charged with criminal facilitation of first-degree sexual abuse, facilitation of menacing, and third-degree criminal abuse.[18] They are also required by law to report suspected abuse to the proper authorities. In addition to the legal ramifications of abuse, lawsuits and loss of reputation are possible consequences.

Reducing the Likelihood of Victimization

1. Develop, follow, and enforce policies and procedures for all activities, including the following:
   a. Bathroom policies: Two adults should take them.
   b. Sick child policies
   c. Child transfer authorization

    d. Who is authorized to work with them and how they are screened

    e. Late/early arrivals and departure policies

    f. Discipline issues

    g. Absent child policies

    h. Drug and alcohol policy

    i. Reporting abuse or inappropriate conduct

    j. How parents can report abuse or inappropriate conduct

2. Rules for youth camps, gyms, and trips

    a. "No one plays alone" rules[19]

    b. Approved adults must be present during all activities.

    c. Rules for showers and locker room

    d. Rules for co-ed activities

    e. Dress code should be posted and signed by each individual.

    f. Definition of inappropriate behaviors

    g. Signed parental consent forms

3. Restrict the access of the following types of unauthorized individuals to children[20]:

    a. Strangers

    b. Non-sanctioned workers or volunteers

    c. Noncustodial parents

    d. Family or friends who are not on the approved pick-up list

    e. Older youth involved with the children's ministry, to minimize the chances of peer-to-peer abuse

4. Screening of staff and volunteers

    a. Establish a standardized application process for all employees and volunteers.[21]

    b. Criminal background checks, keeping the following in mind:

        - Application forms must be verified and references must be checked.

        - Checks cannot verify whether a person is trustworthy or appropriate to work with children.

        - Many sexual offenders might not have a criminal record, so they might not be exposed through a criminal history check.[22]

    c. Child abuse/neglect screening is essential as many states have a separate reporting agency for investigations of child abuse.[23] A person may have been accused and investigated, but not criminally prosecuted.

    d. Remove individuals with negative results on checks.

    e. Conduct a personal interview including the following questions: why they want to work with children; any relevant past issues such as being a victim of abuse; and their philosophy of discipline.[24]

5. Application of effective controls such as record-keeping, accountability, oversight, and supervision.[25]

6. A person should have the designated responsibility of safety-related management and monitoring of all aspects of children and youth ministry.[26]

7. All workers (staff or volunteers) should be trained in all safety-related precautions and procedures.[27] This should include first aid training as well as training in policies and procedures.

8. Drop-off and pick-up procedures should contain a system of identification, such as a child tag system and sign-in/sign-out logs with date, time, and signature.[28]

9. Establish activity standards.[29]

10. Eliminate danger zones—secluded areas where a child may be taken and abused without being observed.[30]

11. Nurseries, day cares, classrooms, and play areas for children should not be isolated from the rest of the building. They should be observable though windows (and cameras, if possible). They should also be located near areas that people frequent.

12. Require at least a six-month waiting period on child supervision for new volunteers.[31]
13. Enhance visibility of activities, including using rooms with windows and keeping doors open.[32]
14. Monitor activities, including making periodic and unannounced drop-ins.[33]
15. Stay cognizant of signs of physical and emotional abuse.[34]
16. Install CCTV in the nursery, day care, and school.[35] Cameras should be installed in prominent locations overlooking primary child care areas, educational areas, and recreation areas.
17. Establish procedures for responding to an accusation. Report it as required and deal with it in a professional manner.[36]
18. Use release and permission forms for outings and potentially high-risk events such as camping or hiking.[37]
19. Discuss policy and needs with an insurance agent and ensure your coverage includes volunteers.[38]
20. Purchase a child-protection program that addresses the safety of children and youth and implement it.[39] Make sure it covers the subject in-depth and includes prevention strategies as well as recovery methods.
21. Consider providing services to crime victims in your community.[40]
22. Child–adult ratios are often governed by state regulations. Ensure that the minimums are followed. However, you should add more adults if you can, provided they perform their duties instead of congregating together.

Standards of Conduct for Staff and Volunteers

Incorporated into your policies and procedures should be standards of conduct for staff and volunteers. Develop a handbook for staff and volunteers including the following:

1. Two adult meeting rule: Ensure that every activity has at least two adults supervising and that they are not related to each other, as sometimes family members collude to victimize children.[41] This includes during transportation by vehicle.
2. One-on-one meetings: If it is not possible to have two adults present, perform the following:
    a. Notify parents and obtain written approval from one parent or guardian.[42]
    b. Try to meet in a public place.
    c. Only meet in the daytime.
    d. Follow any guidelines given by the parents.[43]
3. Classroom doors should remain open unless there are windows in the door.[44]
4. Open door counseling: Keep the door open during counseling sessions. If the meeting must be confidential, the door or room should have a window.
5. Sleepovers and overnight events
    a. Obtain signed permission slips.
    b. There should be a minimum of two adult chaperones.
    c. As long as a child is awake, an adult must be awake.
    d. Adults cannot share sleeping bags or beds with children or youth even their own.
    e. Children or youth should not share beds or sleeping bags.
    f. Wear modest sleeping attire and do not change clothes in front of children or youth.[45]
    g. Have separate sleeping quarters for males and females.
    h. Keep an information sheet on each individual with emergency contact and medical information.

6. Establish guidelines for appropriate displays of affection
7. Establish guidelines for appropriate verbal interaction
8. It is the staff and volunteers' duty to report, but not investigate, suspicious behavior. "Good faith" reporting protects the individual from both civil and criminal liability[46]

Following these guidelines can also provide protection against false accusations, which can be almost as devastating to an organization's reputation as a criminal act.

Be wary of staff or volunteers who exhibit the following characteristics:

- Has special or favorite children or youth
- Spends time with a select few
- Spends free time with a few individuals and invites them for sleepovers
- Gives gifts and special attention to certain individuals
- Engages in inappropriate displays of affection and/or verbal interaction.
- Frequently gives certain individuals rides home
- "Be suspicious of any person who wants to spend time alone with children and would prefer that other adults not be there."[47]
- Frequent physical contact between adults and children
- A youth becoming increasingly dependent on one particular adult[48]
- "Open defiance of a written standard of behavior by the staff member or volunteer, and minimizing of action when confronted"[49]
- "A defensive attitude or questioning of behavior standards by the adult leader when the subject of possible misconduct is raised"[50]

Prevention Strategies

As part of your community outreach, your facility is in a good position to provide resources to parents and children. You can educate your members and attendees on proper parenting skills and abuse prevention. Common activities include the following:

- Public awareness campaigns—including public service announcements (PSAs), posters, and brochures—that promote healthy parenting, child safety, and how to report suspected maltreatment[51]
- Skills-based training courses for children and youth that teach them safety and protection skills and how to report inappropriate behavior[52]
- Parent education programs centered on developing positive parenting skills and decreasing behaviors associated with child abuse and neglect[53]
- Home visiting programs that provide support and assistance to expecting and new mothers[54]
- Mentor or leadership programs that provide role models and support to families in crisis[55]
- Parent support groups for strengthening their families and building social networks[56]
- Respite and crisis care programs that offer temporary relief to caregivers in stressful situations by providing short-term care for their children[57]
- Your facility can become a family resource center, which works with community members to develop a variety of services to meet the specific needs of the people who live in surrounding neighborhoods.[58]

- Special programs that provide education, support, and assistance to families with special needs' children
- Education programs on issues of abuse facilitated by experts in the field and representatives from the state authority for protecting children and families[59]

Handling Allegations and Incidents

Any allegations of misconduct should be immediately and thoroughly investigated. If a staff member or volunteer commits a crime against children or youth, you need to handle the situation promptly. If the accused is a staff member or volunteer, they should be removed from their position until the investigation is complete. Cooperate with law enforcement in any investigation and criminal prosecution.

Individuals who commit crimes must be held accountable, but the organization needs to take some responsibility as well. Appearing to ignore or dismiss the incident will be detrimental to the organization and destroy reputations, not to mention the consequences it will have for the accuser and their family.

The media will likely become involved once allegations are made. A statement should be issued through the media spokesperson. Refer to Chapter 12 for ways to handle the media.

If the incident has occurred at your facility, it is necessary to review, evaluate, and update policies and procedures to ensure that corrective action is taken and preventive measures are instituted. A meeting should be held for members to denounce the occurrence, to explain steps taken up to this point, and outline future preventative measures.[60] Afterward, you may wish to hold a public meeting for those interested that explains the actions the organization has taken to correct the problem and prevent future issues.

Institute staff and volunteer training programs on safety topics including signs of abuse and neglect, appropriate and inappropriate behavior, legal reporting requirements, and organizational policies and procedures. Prevention training should be provided to members and the community as well. Counseling should be provided—whether by your leaders or mental health professionals—to these affected by the crisis.

Handling Allegations

1. Investigate promptly and thoroughly.
2. If a staff member or a volunteer is involved, remove them from duty until the investigation is complete.
3. Issue a statement through the media spokesperson.
4. Hold an organizational meeting on corrective action and prevention.
5. Have a public meeting on corrective action and prevention.
6. Cooperate with the law enforcement investigation and prosecution.
7. Conduct staff, volunteer, and community training programs.
8. Review, evaluate, and update policies and procedures as necessary.
9. Provide counseling.

Final Thoughts

Although it may be difficult to accept, good intentions will not negate potential criminal occurrences or prevent criminal activities. You have an obligation to protect the most vulnerable users of your facility. Most states have mandatory reporting laws as well.

A significant body of ongoing research shows the consequences of child abuse and neglect as being mild or severe; disappearing after a short period or lasting a lifetime; and affecting the child physically, psychologically, behaviorally, or in some combination of all three ways.[61] Factors that affect the consequences are the circumstances of the abuse or neglect, the personal characteristics of the child, and the environment.[62]

Ultimately, due to related costs to public entities such as the health-care, human services, and educational systems, abuse and neglect impact not just the child and family but society as a whole. Therefore, it is imperative for communities to provide a framework of prevention strategies and services before abuse and neglect occur and be prepared to offer remediation and treatment when necessary.

Be proactive and implement strong prevention strategies. Take all allegations seriously and cooperate with law enforcement investigations and prosecution. Most importantly, work together to ensure the safety and security of your most vulnerable attendees.

End Notes

1. Hanna J. W., *Safe and Secure: The Alban Guide to Protecting Your Congregation* (Durham: Alban Institute, 1999).
2. Crabtree J., *Better Safe Than Sued: Keeping Your Students and Ministry Alive* (Grand Rapids: The Livingstone Corporation, 2009).
3. Ibid.
4. Ibid.
5. Ibid.
6. Ibid.
7. Ibid.
8. Carcara W. S., *Advising Houses of Worship on a Comprehensive and Balanced Security Plan* (2009). Retrieved from www.policechiefmagazine.org/magazine/index.cfm?fuseaction=display_arch&article_id=1845&issue_id=72009.
9. Ibid.
10. The GuideOne Center for Risk Management, *The Missing Ministry: Safety, Risk Management, and Protecting Your Church* (Loveland: Group Publishing, Inc., 2008).
11. Aguiar R., *Keeping Your Church Safe* (Maitland: Xulon Press, 2008).
12. Ibid.
13. Cirtin R. M., *Church Safety and Security* (Lima: CSS Publishing Company, 2005).
14. See note 11 above.
15. See note 13 above.
16. See note 11 above.
17. See note 11 above.
18. Quarles C. L. and Ratliff P. L., *Crime Prevention for Houses of Worship* (Alexandria: American Society for Industrial Security, 2001).
19. Ibid.

20. See note 8 above.
21. See note 8 above.
22. See note 8 above.
23. See note 13 above.
24. See note 13 above.
25. See note 8 above.
26. See note 8 above.
27. See note 8 above.
28. See note 8 above.
29. See note 8 above.
30. See note 10 above.
31. See note 8 above.
32. See note 8 above.
33. See note 8 above.
34. See note 8 above.
35. See note 18 above.
36. See note 1 above.
37. See note 1 above.
38. See note 1 above.
39. See note 1 above.
40. See note 1 above.
41. See note 13 above.
42. See note 2 above.
43. See note 2 above.
44. See note 10 above.
45. See note 2 above.
46. See note 13 above.
47. See note 18 above, p. 130.
48. See note 2 above.
49. See note 2 above, p. 58.
50. See note 2 above, p. 58.
51. https://www.childwelfare.gov/pubs/factsheets/preventingcan.pdf#page=2&view=Prevention%20Strategies.
52. Ibid.
53. Ibid.
54. Ibid.
55. Ibid.
56. Ibid.
57. Ibid.
58. Ibid.
59. See note 13 above.
60. See note 11 above.
61. https://www.childwelfare.gov/pubs/factsheets/long_term_consequences.pdf#page=7&view=Summary.
62. Ibid.

Conclusion and Summary

In the United States, we are very fortunate that we do not experience the bombings of religious institutions frequently seen in other parts of the world. However, we do experience crimes of various types in and around our facilities.

Unfortunately, there is no single strategy or preventive countermeasure that will guarantee a religious institution, its employees, or its members will remain untouched by a traumatic incident. However, following the policies outlined in this book will reduce overall risk and mitigate damages.

Religious leaders need to be proactive in protecting their organization. You are encouraged to take safety and security seriously by adopting and adapting the policies, procedures, processes, and practices outlined in this book.

One source of information not previously discussed in detail is the internet. However, caution must be used as some information is not verifiable and some documents have been known to be unreliable at best and faked at worst. Therefore, it is best to use federal or state government websites, as they are most likely to be accurate. Industry associations are another source of accurate information.

There is a saying that the adversary only has to be right once to be successful, while security has to be right all of the time. This means the policies and procedures must be followed correctly every single time to successfully prevent incidents. There should be consistency in application as well as enforcement of compliance.

Although risk mitigation is important, it should not interfere with the activities of the religious institution. It should complement their mission instead. If a balance between security needs and mission needs is not maintained, noncompliance, resentment, and resistance are likely.

Security is not a one-size-fits-all proposition. Each facility has unique vulnerabilities, strengths, and needs that must be accounted for in order to properly secure it. As a result, it is imperative that a thorough risk assessment is conducted.

In addition, threats change as new technologies emerge and changes occur in the social, political, cultural, and economic climate. Therefore, security requires constant review and evaluation of its components and updates as necessary. Security is not a stagnant concept.

While this book provides guidance on security countermeasures, executive protection, and the use of less lethal and lethal weapons, it is not meant to bestow expertise in these areas to the religious institution. Professionals should be consulted and contracted with to handle these serious issues.

Remember, a lifetime of charitable works can be destroyed in an instant by a negative incident involving the facility, its leaders, or its members. The resulting media scrutiny can destroy even if the allegations and accusations are later proven false. Protect your organization by taking security seriously.

Index

Note: Page numbers followed by "b," and "f" indicate boxes, and figures, respectively.